Series / Number 07-039

INTRODUCTION TO APPLIED DEMOGRAPHY

Data Sources and Estimation Techniques

NORFLEET W. RIVES, Jr.
Rice Center
and
University of Delaware

WILLIAM J. SEROW
Florida State University

SAGE PUBLICATIONS
The Publishers of Professional Social Science
Newbury Park London New Delhi

Printed in the United States of America

For information address:

SAGE Publications, Inc.
2111 West Hillcrest Drive
Newbury Park, California 91320

SAGE Publications Ltd.
28 Banner Street
London EC1Y 8QE
England

SAGE Publications India Pvt. Ltd.
M-32 Market
Greater Kailash I
New Delhi 110 048 India

International Standard Book Number 0-8039-2134-9

Library of Congress Catalog Card No. 84-050001

FOURTH PRINTING, 1989

When citing a professional paper, please use the proper form. Remember to cite the correct Sage University Paper series title and include the paper number. One of the following formats can be adapted (depending on the style manual used):

(1) IVERSEN, GUDMUND R. and NORPOTH, HELMUT (1976) "Analysis of Variance." Sage University Paper series on Quantitative Application in the Social Sciences, 07-001. Beverly Hills and London: Sage Pubns.

OR

(2) Iversen, Gudmund R. and Norpoth, Helmut. 1976. *Analysis of Variance.* Sage University Paper series on Quantitative Applications in the Social Sciences, series no. 07-001. Beverly Hills and London: Sage Pubns.

CONTENTS

Series Editor's Introduction

Changing demographic conditions constitute a potent force in contemporary society, continually reshaping the environment in which both the public and private sectors must produce and distribute goods and services to satisfy human demands and needs. Responding to these conditions, businesses and government agencies are beginning to recognize the importance of demographic skills to the success of marketing and strategic planning. No longer can one expect to find demography only at academic institutions, the Bureau of the Census, and the Bureau of Labor Statistics. Increasingly one can expect to find demographers (or persons with demographic skills) on the staffs of state and local governments and a diverse set of public and private establishments.

The growing presence of demographic issues and demographers in business and government operations is largely responsible for the emergence of the field of applied demography. A principal function of the applied demographer is to identify changing demographic conditions and interpret their consequences for the production and distribution of both public and private goods and services. In this capacity, applied demographers monitor the growth, demographic and socioeconomic composition, and geographic distribution of the population of states and local areas. While applied demographers also follow trends in population at the national level, much of their work is concerned with smaller geographic units, such as counties, minor civil divisions, and census tracts. The planning and reporting requirements of businesses and government agencies frequently involve demographic information with greater geographic detail. One major advantage of the small-area approach is the isolation of particular market segments and target populations for more extensive research and analysis, the end result being a more thorough understanding of changing patterns of market demand.

This volume is one of the first on demographic methods to be directed specifically to those with applied interests—both students of the subject and practitioners. In this volume Rives and Serow bring together the essential elements of applied demography in a clear and concise manner. The focus of the volume is demographic information: What kinds of data are available, who produces these data, where one can obtain them, and how they can be used in estimation producers to produce new data. Understanding the structure and sources of demographic information is one of the keys to effective applied demographic analysis.

Chapter 1 provides an introduction to the study of applied demography, emphasizing both the circumstances that are largely responsible for the rapid growth of the field and the particular shape the field has assumed. Chapters 2, 3, and 4 cover the major sources of demographic information. The principal source, the decennial census of population and housing, is examined in considerable detail. Three separate chapters are devoted to information sources to emphasize the central role these sources play in applied demographic work. Chapters 5 and 6 address the production of current demographic estimates with alternative estimation procedures. The focus of both chapters is the preparation of demographic estimates for small geographic areas. Chapter 5 covers alternative methods appropriate for estimating total population. Chapter 6 deals with issues in the estimation of demographic characteristics. Two appendices contain valuable reference resources: a detailed bibliography and a state-by-state tabulation of agencies and organizations that supply demographic statistics.

The mathematical sophistication of applied demography, in general (and this monograph, in particular), is nothing more than elementary algebra. The subject matter can become mechanically tedious, however, especially during the discussion of estimation techniques; and the reader is cautioned about the importance of attention to detail. To ease the burden, the authors use interrelated numerical examples to show precisely how each estimation technique can be employed.

Students of applied demography, notably those in business and economics, demography and the social sciences, urban and regional planning, and public affairs, as well as practitioners in all areas of market research and planning, will find Rives and Serow's *Introduction to Applied Demography* a welcome and useful volume.

—*Richard G. Niemi*
Series Co-Editor

Acknowledgments

The authors gratefully acknowledge the partial financial support of the Houston/Independent Research Program in the preparation of this volume. Established by the Rice Center Board of Directors with generous contributions from the Houston business and civic communities, The H/IRP program is designed to assist local business and government leaders to identify and evaluate significant issues that will confront Houston over the next several decades.

The authors also gratefully acknowledge the valuable technical assistance of Harold Goldsmith, National Institute of Mental Health, whose comments on an earlier draft of the manuscript are largely responsible for the organization of this volume.

INTRODUCTION TO APPLIED DEMOGRAPHY
Data Sources and Estimation Techniques

NORFLEET W. RIVES, Jr.
Rice Center and University of Delaware

WILLIAM J. SEROW
Florida State University

1. INTRODUCTION TO APPLIED DEMOGRAPHY

Demography is the scientific study of human populations. As such, demography is concerned with decisions individuals make regarding matters like marriage, childbearing, place of residence, and place of work, and whether these choices vary among different population groups, groups defined in terms of innate characteristics such as sex and race, and acquired economic and social characteristics such as occupational status and educational attainment. Demography can be purely descriptive, stating, for example, what has happened to the size or composition of population, without attempting to explain these changes. Demography can also be analytical, stating, for example, what the causal nexus might be between the educational and occupational choices women make on the one hand, and their marital and childbearing choices on the other. In essence, then, demographers seek to explore the determinants and consequences of human population change.

The Scope and Content of Applied Demography

Within the broader framework of demography there has probably always existed a specialization that we have only recently begun to call "applied demography." The term itself is so new that there is no one definition that would be generally accepted by all who profess to be applied demographers. In our view, applied demography is that branch of the discipline that is directed toward the production, dissemination, and analysis of demographic and closely related socioeconomic information for quite specific purposes of planning and reporting. To distinguish "applied" pursuits from other lines of demographic inquiry, we would further suggest that applied demography is more concerned with the measurement and interpretation of current and prospective population change than with the behavioral determinants of this change. While many lines of demographic inquiry involve the analysis of statistical information pertaining to individuals, families, and households, applied demography almost always deals with information on population size, growth, and composition for specific geographic areas. Thus there is an identifiable difference in the unit of analysis: Applied demographers tend to focus on geographic units and their population characteristics, while others are more concerned with individuals and their demographic behavior.

Much of the work of applied demography over the past two or three decades has involved the area of population estimation and projection. The one topic within this area that dominates the technical landscape is the measurement and analysis of migration. The interest that applied demographers have shown for migration research is quite understandable. Migration is the principal component of demographic change for state and local areas, and the migration component at these levels of geography is quite difficult to measure. Since most population estimates and projections are prepared for small geographic units, their accuracy reflects to a great degree the quality of migration information.

Several developments of the past 10 to 15 years point to the emergence of applied demography as a legitimate field of inquiry. One of the most significant developments is the Federal-State Cooperative Program for Population Estimates. Established by the Bureau of the Census in the late 1960s as a joint venture with the states, this program formally recognized population estimation for states and counties as an important demographic activity of the federal government. During more recent years other cooperative population programs have come into existence, further strengthening the position of applied demography in the public sector. We will be discussing some of these programs in greater detail in Chapter 2.

A second major development is the spread of applied demography to business. Interest within the private sector reflects the rapid growth of business planning and reporting requirements. More and more firms have begun to appreciate the importance of knowing and understanding the "demographics" of a particular situation or potential market.

Indeed, a small industry of private companies has emerged whose principal line of business is to provide these demographics to other firms. While other factors still dictate most business decisions, few large corporations, especially those in consumer goods, would seriously consider marketing a new product, opening a new branch, or moving to a new location without first investigating demographic issues. The future of applied demography in business circles would seem to be quite promising.

A third major development is the greater recognition of applied demographic pursuits within the larger community of professional demographers. The Population Association of America, the principal national society of professional demographers, has had a standing committee on state and local demography for several years, and the society recently established a permanent committee on business demography. The Southern Regional Demographic Group, the most prominent regional professional organization in the field, has established its own committee on applied demography. Both societies now sponsor scientific paper sessions on applied demographic issues at their annual meetings, to provide students and practitioners with the opportunity to exchange ideas on topics of current interest.

Demography is fortunate to have its own comprehensive bibliographic publication. *Population Index*, available to the larger community of professional demographers for nearly 50 years, provides bibliographic citations and abstracts to the literature on population published in many languages around the world. Printed copies of *Population Index* are issued on a quarterly basis and may be found in series at most college and university libraries. All types of material, both published and unpublished, appear in *Population Index*. The bibliographic classifications of particular interest to applied demographers include

(1) spatial distribution;
(2) trends in population growth and size;
(3) migration;
(4) methods of research and analysis, including models;
(5) the production of population statistics;
(6) official statistical publications;
(7) machine-readable data files.

Each *Population Index* citation contains complete bibliographic information and a descriptive abstract.

Organization of this Volume

The materials and techniques of applied demography can be viewed simultaneously from two perspectives: geographic and temporal. Each perspective affords two distinct alternatives. The geographic perspective is the dichotomy between large and small areas. By "large" areas, we generally mean states, groups of states, and the nation as a whole, and by "small" areas, we generally mean counties (or their equivalent), municipalities, and various subcounty entities, such as minor civil divisions (often called townships) and census tracts.

The temporal perspective is the dichotomy between the census year and all other years. A census year is one during which a complete enumeration of the population is undertaken. In the United States the decennial census is conducted in years ending in zero.

If we consider the routine availability of demographic information within the framework of the two perspectives just outlined, we arrive at the following matrix of data sources:

Temporal Perspective	Large Areas	Small Areas
Census Year	Decennial Census	Decennial Census
Other Year	Current Surveys	Current Estimates

The purpose of this handbook is to present fundamental concepts and methods associated with each of the elements of applied demography shown in this matrix. We do not claim that these pages cover everything one needs to know about the subject, but we do think that we have assembled a useful document for both students and practitioners seeking an introduction to basic concepts and methods.

We have divided the remainder of this volume into five chapters. The first two are concerned with sources of demographic statistics. We believe that every applied demographer should be conversant with those statistical programs that provide the nucleus of demographic information. Chapter 2 discusses the backbone of the demographic information system—the decennial census— and Chapter 3 covers current surveys, which provide most of the demographic data for large areas in noncensus years. Chapter 4 introduces the vital registration system, an important supplement to the larger demographic information system. Together, the data sources described in these three chapters form the empirical basis for the estimation techniques required to complete the matrix.

The final three chapters of this volume deal with the methodology of estimation. Chapter 5 introduces elementary techniques for estimating total population, which we consider an essential skill for applied demographic work. In this chapter we also mention, briefly, more sophisticated procedures for producing estimates of population. Chapter 6 raises the general issue of the rationale for estimates of demographic detail—age, sex, race/ethnicity, and income—for planning and reporting, and presents an illustrative example of a basic procedure for producing such detail.

As a final note, we want to call attention to the fact that this volume deals solely with current estimates of population and not with demographic forecasts. While there undoubtedly exists the need for a volume comparable to this one on forecasting, space considerations alone preclude a substantive treatment of this topic here. The reader who is comfortable with comparatively sophisticated methodologies should consult Pittenger (1976) and Irwin (1977) on population projection.

2. CENSUS STATISTICS

The 1980 Census of Population and Housing is the twentieth decennial enumeration of the United States. The first took place in 1790, and one has been conducted every decade since, always in a year ending in zero. The Constitution provides for these enumerations, to reapportion the House of Representatives.

The official date of the 1980 census is April 1. Every census since 1930 has been conducted officially on this date. Experience indicates that April is one time of the year when most of the population can be found at home. Finding people at home is important because the enumeration basis for the census is "usual place of residence," usual in the sense that a person resides there most of the year. Rules have been developed for determining usual place of residence in those special situations in which a person lives in more than one place during the course of a year, and the choice of a "usual" place of residence is not so obvious.

The 1980 census was conducted by the Bureau of the Census, an agency of the United States Department of Commerce, with headquarters in Suitland, Maryland, a suburb of Washington. The bureau has conducted every census since 1910. Earlier censuses were handled by a temporary office, established prior to each census and dismantled after the census work had been completed. It was not until 1902 that Congress decided to create a permanent census organization.

The decennial census, for all practical purposes, is a statistical portrait of the nation. Census portraits over the years have grown increasingly complex, as information demands have become more sophisticated. The 1980 census offers what many consider the most detailed portrait ever produced. To appreciate the importance of the census portrait to applied demographic analysis, it is necessary to understand what kind of information the decennial census contains, the system of geographic areas for which census information is reported, and the program of publications, data products, and special services the Census Bureau provides to facilitate the use of census results. Beyond these essential items, it is also useful to know something about the errors to which census data are subject, and the means the bureau has to updata census information to noncensus years.

Census Subjects

The subject coverage of the decennial census has changed dramatically over the years. Differences between earlier censuses and those of more recent generations reflect the changing interests and information needs of the nation. Emphasis has moved from detailed personal inventories, typical of the first enumerations, to broad statistical accountings for items—such as housing, employment, income, transportation, education—that provide the empirical basis for planning and public policy at all levels of society.

Comparing census inquiries on the first and most recent enumerations can illustrate just how significant the changes in subject coverage have been. Conducted by marshals of the United States judicial districts, the 1790 census is basically an enumeration of population. The 1790 schedule required a marshal to list the name of the head of the family and the number of persons in each household of the following descriptions:

(1) free white males aged 16 and over,

(2) free white males under age 16,

(3) free white females,

(4) all other free persons, and

(5) slaves.

The 1980 census also is an enumeration of population, in keeping with the constitutional mandate, but any similarity between the first and most recent census really ends here. Table 2-1 shows the subject coverage of the 1980 census. The 1790 schedule, with its emphasis on broad population groups, stands in stark contrast to the 1980 schedule, with its richness of subject detail. The growth and development of census information from 1790 to 1980 follows an interesting progression. The Census Bureau has compiled an excellent account of the history of these inquiries (U.S. Bureau of the Census, 1979a).

The 1980 census schedule is divided along two lines. Population items are distinguished from housing items, and 100 percent items are distinguished from sample items. Both distinctions warrant further explanation. The first distinction ostensibly reflects the dichotomous nature of the subject matter, but the major point is that the modern decennial census is really two censuses in one. There is a census for population, which covers demographic, economic, and social characteristics of individuals and households, and a technically separate census of housing, which covers equipment, financial, and structural characteristics of housing units. The two censuses, which are the responsibility of different administrative divisions at the Census Bureau, are conducted concurrently for obvious reasons.

The second distinction involves the way in which census information is now collected. Prior to 1950, taking the census meant canvassing every house in every neighborhood in the country. This approach is what most people have in mind when someone speaks of a census "enumeration." Indeed, the Constitution mandates the counting of population for reapportionment. Starting with the 1950 census, the Census Bureau turned to the scientific technique of sampling to collect certain information on population and housing characteristics. Sampling has a tremendous comparative advantage over complete enumeration as a method of data collection in large populations. The cost associated with the loss in accuracy as a consequence of sampling is more than offset by the substantial cost saving associated with the use of sampling, rather than a complete count, to collect information.

The particular sample design associated with the decennial census permits the bureau to realize significant benefits from sampling, while satisfying the constitutional requirement that the population actually be counted. The design involves the use of two different census questionnaires. One contains only those subject items in Table 2-1 identified as 100 percent items; the version of the questionnaire is commonly called the "short form." The other contains both 100 percent and sample items;

this version is called the "long form." In the 1980 census a long form went to approximately one out of every five households in the nation, thus creating roughly a 20 percent sample of sample population and housing items. A sampling fraction of this magnitude is sufficient to provide good statistical reliability in census results for small geographic areas. Since the number of persons in each household in still actually counted under the two-questionnaire sample design, the constitutional requirement for a population enumeration is satisfied.

One final point concerning census subject coverage deserves attention. The items shown in Table 2-1 represent the consensus of a number of individuals and organizations concerning the content of the 1980 census. These items do not reflect just the interests and preferences of persons who work at the Census Bureau. By law, Congress has the final decision on the content of the census schedule. As part of the advance planning for a census, the bureau holds public hearings around the country to solicit suggestions for possible census items. Proposals also can be made at these hearings to delete items from the schedule and to modify census procedures. Each new item proposed is subsequently evaluated to determine its suitability as a census subject. An item typically does not make the schedule for one of several reasons: Data appropriate to the matter at hand can be obtained routinely from other sources; the item is not easily measured through the use of one or two self-administered questions; or the item does not involve the reporting of factual (in principle, verifiable) information, but rather concerns attitudes, opinions, or other expressions of behavior. Many of the items that appear on the census schedule are required by one or more agencies of the federal government for the operation of domestic assistance programs; some of the basic demographic items, like age, sex, and ethnicity, are required by programs almost too numerous to count.

Census Geography

The changing structure of census geography over the years closely parallels the changing scope of census subjects. At the same time the demand for more subject detail has grown, so has the demand for greater geographic detail. Decennial censuses through 1840 did not involve a formal requirement that the results be tabulated for specific geographic areas. Beyond a basic count of population, census marshals were not obligated to summarize returns for states, counties, or cities, although some chose to do so. The first explicit recognition of geographic detail came with the 1850 census. The regulations governing

TABLE 2-1
1980 Census Subject Coverage

100 PERCENT ITEMS

Population	Housing
Household relationship	Number of units at address
Sex	Complete plumbing facilities
Race	Number of rooms
Age	Tenure (whether unit is owned or rented)
Marital status	Condominium identification
Spanish/Hispanic origin or descent	Value of home (owner-occupied units and condominiums)
	Contract rent (renter-occupied units)
	Vacant for rent, for sale, and period of vacancy

SAMPLE ITEMS

Population	Housing
School enrollment	Type of unit
Educational attainment	Stories in building and presence of elevator
State or foreign country of birth	Year built
Citizenship and year of immigration	Year moved into this house
Current language and English proficiency	Acreage and crop sales
Ancestry	Source of water
Place of residence five years ago	Sewage disposal
Activity five years ago	Heating equipment
Veteran status and period of service	Fuels used for house heating, water heating, and cooking
Presence of disability or handicap	Costs of utilities and fuels
Children ever born	Complete kitchen facilities
Marital history	Number of bedrooms
Employment status last week	Number of bathrooms
Hours worked last week	Telephone
Place of work	Air conditioning
Travel time to work	Number of automobiles
Means of transportation to work	Number of light trucks and vans
Persons in carpool	Homeowner shelter costs for mortgages, real estate taxes, and hazard insurance
Year last worked	
Industry	
Occupation	
Class of worker	
Weeks looking for work in 1979	
Amount of income in 1979 by source	

this enumeration required census marshals to divide their districts into "known civil divisions" for reporting purposes. These divisions typically took the form of counties, townships, and wards—areas with reasonably easily identifiable boundaries. The growth and development of census geography beyond this initial requirement follows a fairly steady progression through the 1980 census toward substantially greater geographic detail. Once divided primarily into broad political jurisdictions for the purpose of taking a census, the nation has now been carved into thousands of minor administrative and statistical areas for which census results can be reported.

Figure 2-1 presents the system of geographic areas used in conjuction with the 1980 census. Three panels of this figure illustrate the hierarchical relations that exist among areas. Panels A and C provide a broad overview of geographic structure for the nation as a whole, while Panel B focuses on the structure of metropolitan areas, where most people now reside.

Beginning with panel A, one can see that the country is divided initially into regions, divisions, states, and counties. States are subdivided further into congressional districts and places, and counties, into minor civil divisions, or census county divisions, and enumeration districts or block groups. There are four census regions and nine divisions. These areas are basically groups of states and historically have been useful for charting the movement of population westward over the past century. Regions and divisions are special statistical areas, as the key to Figure 2-1 indicates. They serve no official function, and beyond providing a convenient aggregation scheme for states, they have no real purpose.

States and counties are the two most commonly encountered subdivisions of the nation. Both provide a mutually exclusive, completely exhaustive system of geographic units for the country as a whole. There are 50 states and the District of Columbia, which the Census Bureau treats as a state for census purposes. The number of counties varies only slightly from one census to the next. At the time of the 1980 census there were 3004 counties and 133 areas the bureau designated "county equivalents."[1] The real variation in the number of counties is across states at a point in time. Delaware, one of the smallest states in the nation, has only three counties, while Texas, one of the largest states, has 254!

Continuing with Panel A of Figure 2-1, one can see that both states and counties are further subdivided for census reporting. In addition to

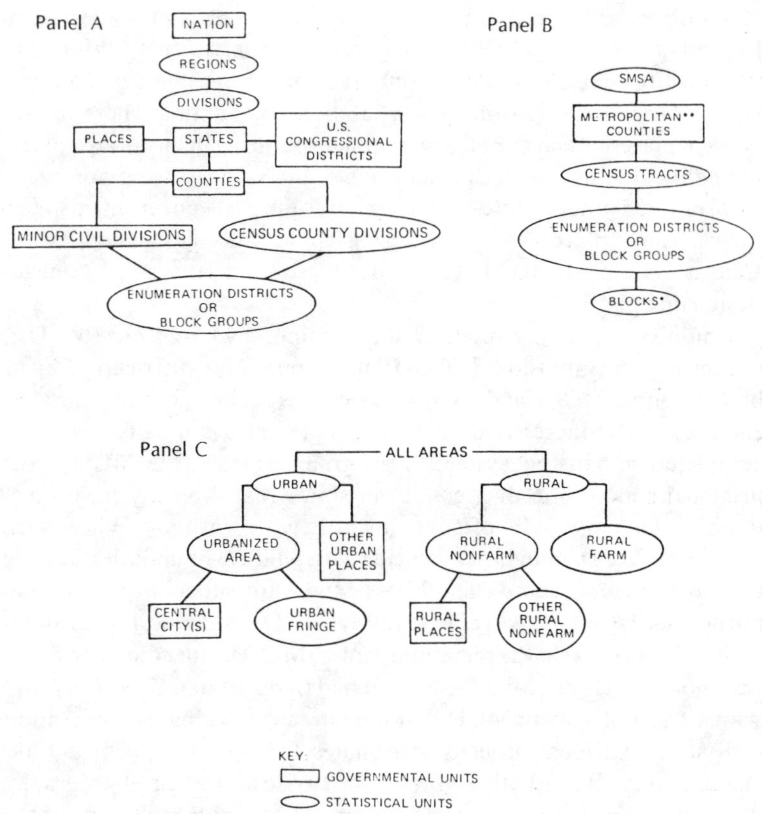

SOURCE: U.S. Bureau of the Census.
*Blocks cover only the urbanized area of an SMSA.
**In New England, metropolitan towns (MCDs) and cities replace counties as the components of SMSAs.

Figure 2-1 Census Geography—Hierarchical Structure of Units

the subdivision into counties, states are divided into congressional districts and places. Congressional districts—another mutually exclusive, completely exhaustive system of geographic units—constitute the areas served by members of the House of Representatives. District boundaries are subject to change once every decade, when another decennial census provides new information on the geographic distribution of population, and many boundaries, especially those of districts in rapidly growing or declining areas, are actually adjusted. Revising congressional districts to give each member of the House of Representatives roughly the same number of constituents conforms to the constitutional principle of equal representation ("one person, one vote"). The place is the other major subdivision of a state. There are two types of places—incorporated and unincorporated. Incorporated places are political units—such as cities, towns, and villages—that are legally incorporated under state law as general-purpose governments. Unincorporated places are special geographic units designated by the Census Bureau. In the 1980 census, these units are called "census-designated places."

Counties are further subdivided into minor civil divisions (MCDs), or census county divisions (CCDs), and enumeration districts (EDs), or block groups. MCDs and CCDs, like census regions, divisions, states, counties, and congressional districts, represent a mutually exclusive, completely exhaustive system of geographic areas. The MCD is the principal subdivision of a county in states that typically have functioning subcounty units of government (e.g., townships). Where such units exist, MCD boundaries coincide with political boundaries, and the Census Bureau can conveniently use MCDs for subcounty tabulation purposes. The bureau was able to follow MCD designations in 29 states in the 1980 census. In the remaining states, MCDs either did not exist or were not well defined, and the bureau had to resort to CCDs. The CCD is an area similar to an MCD that the bureau, working in cooperation with state and local officials, designates for census reporting. Enumeration districts and block groups, the two lowest levels of geography shown in Panel A, are designed primarily to facilitate the taking of the census. Both are special statistical areas for which the Census Bureau publishes some information. Apart from the opportunity they offer for small-area tabulation, EDs, and block groups are not very useful for demographic analysis.

Panel B of Figure 2-1 contains some of the most popular census geography—popular because most Americans live in metropolitan areas and statistics for these areas are in high demand. At the base of hierarchy for metropolitan census geography is the Standard Metropolitan Statistical Area (SMSA). Unlike other segments of census geography, which are defined either by the Census Bureau or by state and local governments, SMSAs are designated by the Office of Management and Budget (OMB) in Washington, and their boundaries cannot be changed without OMB approval. An SMSA is an integrated economic and social unit with an identifiably large population nucleus. Each SMSA consists generally of one or more counties, or county equivalents, that meet standards pertaining to population and metropolitan character. All counties that fall within an SMSA are designated "metropolitan" counties. The standards that govern SMSA definitions are subject to periodic revision; thus the areas themselves can change over time. Just prior to the 1980 census, OMB had designated a total of 288 SMSAs. Postcensal revisions have since driven the number to more than 320. When two or more SMSAs are adjacent and meet certain other requirements, they can be combined to form a Standard Consolidated Statistical Area (SCSA). Thirteen SCSAs had been designated at the time of the 1980 census.

The federal government has been working for a number of years now to develop new criteria for the definition of metropolitan areas. Names like Metropolitan Statistical Area (MSA), Primary Metropolitan Statistical Area (PMSA), and Consolidated Metropolitan Statistical Area (CMSA) are scheduled to replace the SMSA and SCSA conventions. MSAs conceptually resemble the familiar SMSAs they replace. An MSA is a geographic area consisting of a large population nucleus together with adjacent communities having a high degree of economic and social integration with that nucleus. Outside the six New England states and Alaska, counties are the basic building blocks for MSAs, just as they were for SMSAs.

Data users needs to be acquainted not only with MSAs, but also with CMSAs and PSMAs. A CMSA is any MSA of more than one million population that contains at least two areas qualifying for separate recognition as MSAs. A PMSA is a large urbanized county, or cluster of counties, that exhibits very strong economic and social links, in addition to close ties to the other portions of the CMSA. Analysts may find it helpful to think of PMSAs and CMSAs as "partial MSAs" and "complete MSAs." What the federal government has done, essentially, is to identify the largest geographic area that meets MSA criteria. If the 1980 census population of that area exceeds one million, and if the area contains one or more component counties that would have qualified as MSAs had they not been part of the larger MSA, then those smaller subareas have been defined as PMSAs, and the larger MSA has been defined as a CMSA.

The new metropolitan-area criteria incorporate two major improvements over the existing rules. One is purely methodological; the procedure used to designate metropolitan areas now warrants an extensive overhaul. The other is more practical; the boundaries of current SMSAs need to be reconsidered in light of new information from the 1980 census on metropolitan commuting patterns and population density.

Continuing with Panel B of Figure 2-1, one can see that the census tract is the next lower level in the hierarchy of metropolitan geographic units. Census tracts are generally small, relatively permanent areas into which metropolitan counties (and certain nonmetropolitan counties) are divided for the purpose of reporting statistics at the neighborhood level that will have some degree of comparability from one census to the next. Producing census information for different parts of a city is one of the reasons originally behind the tract concept. Census tract boundaries are determined through the cooperative efforts of the Census Bureau and local census committees. Tract definitions must adhere to certain standards that impose limits on population size and require that all boundaries be easily identifiable. Geographic shape and areal size of tracts are less important considerations. While tract boundaries are rarely altered, tracts may be subdivided or aggregated periodically to maintain conformity with Census Bureau guidelines.

All census tracts are divided further into enumeration districts or block groups, and then certain census tracts are divided into blocks. The EDs and block groups are the same areas shown in Panel A of Figure 2-1, and we can dismiss them here for the same reason; their usefulness in demographic analysis is limited. The block is the smallest geographic unit for which census information is reported. Indeed, blocks are so small that tabulations are made only for the 100 percent subject items (Table 2-1); sampling error and the census disclosure restrictions prevent sample items from being reported at the block level. A census block is generally a well-defined parcel of land, bounded by streets, roads, railroad tracks, streams, or other reasonably permanent and easily identifiable physical features. In the more densely populated central city of an SMSA, one can usually expect census blocks to correspond quite closely to city blocks. In rural areas that do not have a clearly defined street pattern, census blocks can be quite large and take on irregular geographic shapes.

More than 2.5 million blocks were designated for the 1980 census. The block statistics program extends automatically to two types of areas: (1) the urbanized area of an SMSA, which includes the central city and the surrounding closely settled areas (urban fringe) that meet certain criteria of population size or density, and (2) an incorporated place of 10,000 inhabitants or more located outside the urbanized area of an SMSA. In addition, local governments may contract with the Census Bureau to have census blocks designated in areas that would not be blocked otherwise. Contract arrangements of this type also can be made for the designation of census tracts in nonmetropolitan counties. The growing demand for small-area demographic statistics led a number of state and local governments to request special block and tract designations for the 1980 census.

Panel C of Figure 2-1 illustrates the hierarchical relation of census geographic units, following various definitions of urban and rural areas. This approach actually dates from a period when the requirements of demographic analysis placed less emphasis on small-area detail, and thus could be satisfied by broader, less precise geographic distinctions. Under the scheme in Panel C, the county can be divided initially into urban and rural areas. The urban population consists of all persons living in (1) incorporated places of 2500 inhabitants or more, (2) census-designated (unincorporated) places of 2500 inhabitants or more, and (3) other territory, incorporated or unincorporated, included within urbanized areas. The population not classified as urban constitutes the rural population. Residents of rural areas belong to either the rural farm population, which comprises all rural households living on farms, or the rural nonfarm population, which comprises the remaining rural households.

The three panels of Figure 2-1 tell most of the story on census geography. Only a few special geographic units remain to be discussed. One is the postal ZIP code area. The United States Postal Service determines ZIP boundaries to facilitate the delivery of mail. The boundaries are revised on a regular basis to accommodate geographic shifts in mail volume. It is only by chance that ZIP code boundaries coincide with the boundaries of other census areas. Despite this problem, however, the demand for ZIP tabulations from the decennial census is substantial. Detailed population and housing information reported for ZIP code areas has numerous applications in business market research and direct-mail marketing operations.

Another special geographic unit is the election precinct. In more recent censuses, the Census Bureau has tabulated statistics for geographic areas that provide a basis for state and local legislative representation. These tabulations are not automatic; governments must request that the work be done and give the bureau maps showing the boundaries of the areas in question. While states must reapportion their legislative bodies at regular intervals, just as they must reconsider their congressional districts every ten years, not all states need special census tabulations to complete the task. Public Law 94-171, passed by the Congress in 1975, requires the Census Bureau to provide population counts at a geographic level sufficient for legislative redistricting, but the law leaves to the discretion of individual states the particular census information they can use in their redistricting work.

A third special geographic unit that warrants discussion is the "state equivalent." Conceptually similar to the county equivalent, state equivalents refer to certain territories that fall under the administrative jurisdiction of the United States government. State equivalents in the 1980 census include the District of Columbia, Puerto Rico, American Samoa, Guam, the Virgin Islands, and the Commonwealth of the Northern Marianas. The territories of the Carribean and the South Pacific were designated "outlying areas" in earlier censuses. Geographic coverage of the decennial census also was extended for the first time in 1980 to all federal and state Indian reservations. Separate tabulations are to be produced for 280 American Indian reservations and 209 Alaska Native villages.

Once boundaries have been established for the multitude of administrative and statistical areas that comprise census geography, current boundary information must be maintained. The bureau simply cannot afford to drop the matter of census geography once a census has been completed, because the system of geographic units that supports the census also plays a role in other government statistical programs, many of which produce information much more frequently than once every ten years. Furthermore, the cost of "starting from scratch" with census geography for each new census would be almost certainly prohibitive. Statistical areas designated by the Census Bureau for the 1980 census will remain in effect until 1990, when the bureau will officially unveil a new system of units incorporating changes made over the decade. Census Bureau personnel work closely with local census committees and state and local officials to develop changes in statistical area boundaries that will facilitate the collection and use of census information. With respect to administrative areas, the bureau conducts the Boundary and Annexation survey at regular intervals to determine what changes have been made in the boundaries of local political units since the last inventory. Governments are responsible for the boundaries of their jurisdiction, and it is in their interest to keep the Census Bureau informed of official revisions of boundary definitions.

Census Products and Services

Decennial censuses generate a substantial amount of statistical information. To facilitate the use of this information in the widest possible range of applications, the Census Bureau has designed an extensive data dissemination program. The scale of the 1980 program attests to the increasing sophistication of users of census information.

The Census Bureau now uses three major media to release census results—printed reports, computer tapes, and microfiche. Despite the growing popularity of computers in census analysis, the bureau continues to produce a large number of printed reports; for the person who has only an occasional need for census information, resorting to the tables in a printed report is still considered a practical approach. The publications of the 1980 census, like those of the 1970 program, are designed for release in three series:

(1) reports from the Census of Population,

(2) reports from the Census of Housing, and

(3) joint Reports from the Census of Population and Housing.

Table 2-2 presents the major reports in each series. Since time is needed following a census to prepare detailed information for final publication, and since the report production schedule can extend over a period of years, the Bureau issues some reports in preliminary and advance versions to give anxious users a chance to begin working more immediately with basic population and housing counts. Preliminary reports appear first, followed by advance reports, and ultimately by final reports.

The publications shown in Table 2-2 are the major reports in each series, not the only reports. The population census series also will include a number of subject and supplementary reports that focus on particular census subjects and present special tabulations for specific population groups. Subject reports in recent censuses have covered topics such as marital status, migration, education, income, and employment. The amount of geographic detail tends to vary from one subject report to another; most reports present some information at the census division level, only a few show statistics for states and larger cities.

In addition to the reports shown in Table 2-2, the housing census series also will include a number of subject and supplementary reports, as well as reports on residential finance and the components of change in the inventory of housing units. The housing subject reports, like their population counterparts, focus on particular topics—the housing of the elderly, mobile homes, and American Indian households, for example. Only one supplementary housing report has been produced to date, a report on selected housing characteristics by states and counties. The two reports on residential finance and components of inventory change are summary reports, containing information only for the United States as a whole and for census regions.

TABLE 2-2
Major Report Series from the 1980 Census

Population	
Series PC(1)-A (one per state)	Number of Inhabitants. Final official population counts are presented for states, counties, SMSAs, urbanized areas, minor civil divisions, census county divisions, all incorporated places, and census designated places of 1000 inhabitants or more.
Series PC(1)-B (one per state)	General Population Characteristics. Statistics on age, sex, race, marital status, Spanish/Hispanic origin, and household relationships are presented for states, counties, SMSAs, urbanized areas, minor civil divisions, census county divisions, Indian reservations, and places of 1000 inhabitants or more.
Series PC(1)-C (one per state)	General Social and Economic Characteristics. These reports focus on population items collected on a sample basis. Each subject is shown for the following areas: states, counties, SMSAs, urbanized areas, and places of 2500 inhabitants or more.
Series PC(1)-D (one per state)	Detailed Characteristics. These reports cover most of the population subjects collected on a sample basis, presenting the data in considerable detail and cross-classified by age, race, and other characteristics. Each subject is shown for the following areas: States (by urban, rural-nonfarm, and rural-farm residence), large SMSAs, and large cities.
Housing	
Series HC(1)-A (one per state)	General Housing Characteristics. Statistics on 100 percent housing items are presented for states, counties, SMSAs, urbanized areas, minor civil divisions, census county divisions, Indian reservations, and places of 1000 inhabitants or more.
Series HC(1)-B (one per state)	Detailed Housing Characteristics. These reports focus on the housing items collected on a sample basis. Each subject is shown for the following areas: states, counties, SMSAs, urbanized areas, and places of 2500 inhabitants or more.
Population and Housing	
Series PHC(1) (one per SMSA and one for each state)	Block Statistics. Reports show data for individual blocks on selected 100 percent population and housing items. The series includes one report for each SMSA (presenting block statistics for the urbanized areas, places of 10,000 inhabitants or more, and smaller communities that contracted with the Census Bureau to provide block statistics) and a "balance of state" report for each state (presenting block statistics for places of 10,000 inhabitants or more outside SMSAs and smaller communities that contracted with the Census Bureau to provide block statistics).

Table 2-2 (Continued)

Series PHC(2) (one per SMSA and one for and state)	Census Tracts. Reports present selected population and housing items (100 percent and sample) for individual census tracts. The series includes one report for each SMSA and a "balance of state" report for those tracted areas outside SMSAs.
Series PHC(3) (one per state)	Summary Characteristics for Governmental Units. Reports present selected population and housing items (100 percent and sample) for counties, incorporated places, and "active" MCDs qualifying for federal revenue sharing assistance.

The number of reports to be issued jointly from the population and housing censuses goes well beyond the three shown in Table 2-2, although these three are the major reports in the series. Current plans call for joint reports on the population and housing characteristics of congressional districts, the completeness of enumeration of the 1980 census and the quality of responses to census questions, and certain administrative and methodological aspects of the 1980 census program. Two major reports in that last category are the *Users' Guide to the 1980 Census of Population and Housing*, an invaluable reference document, and the *1980 Census Procedural History*, a detailed account of the decennial census operation from the first stages of planning through the final stages of data dissemination and evaluation. The joint report series also covers the industrial and occupational classifications adopted for the 1980 census and the numerical coding scheme used for census geographic units.

The 1980 census computer tape program includes five general-purpose summary tape files and a series of special-purpose tape files. The summary tape files (STFs) contain the same type of information found in the major publication series (Table 2-2). One important feature of the STFs is their ability to provide statistics with greater subject and geographic detail than is feasible or desirable to incorporate in printed and microfiche reports. It is simply more economical and efficient to store census information on computer tapes than on printed pages; much more information can be maintained in a much smaller space. The five STFs produced in conjunction with the 1980 census vary with respect to geographic and subject detail. Table 2-3 presents a general description of each summary file.

In addition to the STF series, the 1980 census computer tape program also includes a number of special-purpose files. One is the Master Area Reference File (MARF), an extract of STF-1 designed for those who need a master list of geographic codes and area names, along with basic

TABLE 2-3

1980 Census Summary Computer Tape Files

STF	*Geographic Detail*	*Subject Detail*
1	Blocks, EDs/block groups, census tracts, places, MCDs/CCDs, counties, congressional districts, states, divisions, regions	Basic tabulations of 100 percent items
2	Census tracts, places of 1000 or more inhabitants, MCDs/CCDs, counties, SMSAs, Indian reservations, states, divisions, regions	Detailed tabulations of 100 percent items with separate summaries for race and Spanish/Hispanic categories
3	EDs/block groups, census tracts, MCDs/CCDs, places, counties, ZIP code areas, congressional districts, states, divisions, regions	Basic tabulations of sample items in combination with selected 100 percent items (notably age and race)
4	Census tracts, places of 2500 or more inhabitants, MCDs/CCDs, counties, SMSAs, Indian reservations, states, divisions, regions	Detailed tabulations of sample items in combination with selected 100 percent items (notably age and race) with separate summaries for race and Spanish/Hispanic categories
5	States, SMSAs, large counties and cities (50,000 or more inhabitants)	More detailed tabulations of sample items in combination with selected 100 percent items (notably age and race)

census counts arranged hierarchically from the state down to the ED/block group level. Copies of MARF are issued separately for each state. Another file is the special population summary prepared in accordance with Public Law 94-171. Developed for the purpose of state and local legislative redistricting, this file contains total population, race, and Spanish/Hispanic counts for all areas identified in the 1980 census. Still another special-purpose file is the Census/EEO tabulation, designed for those who need census information for Equal Opportunity Employment and affirmative action applications. This file contains two tabulations, one with detailed occupational information and the other with years of school completed by age. Each tabulation is further broken down by sex and race or Hispanic or origin. The Census/EEO file covers all counties, all SMSAs, and all incorporated places with at least 50,000 inhabitants.

The Public-Use Microdata Samples constitute yet another group of special-purpose files. Each sample is drawn at random from the universe of individual census records and includes most of the population and housing items that appear on the census questionnaire. The microdata files contain no names or addresses, and geographic identification is sufficiently broad to protect the confidentiality of census respondents. There are three mutually exclusive samples for the 1980 census. One is designed to include five percent of all persons and housing units, and the other two are designed to include one percent. The geographic coding scheme developed for the samples permits the identification of states, most large SMSAs, and counties of 100,000 inhabitants or more on at least one of the files. The major advantage of the microdata samples over the summary tape files is the ability to prepare custom tabulations and cross-tabulations; STF tabulation schemes are fixed at the time the files are produced.

One final special-purpose file that definitely warrants discussion is the Geographic Base File/Dual Independent Map Encoding (GBF/DIME) file. The concept is less intimidating than the label. Unlike other special-purpose files we have mentioned, the GBF/DIME file is not a tabulation of census information; it contains no statistics per se on population and housing. What the file does contain is a set of boundary coordinates that serve as reference points in a procedure that assigns census geographic codes to individual street addresses. For all practical purposes, the GBF/DIME file is a computerized version of a detailed street map. The process for assigning geographic codes to addresses is called geocoding. An illustration should help to clarify the concept.

Consider the set of medical records that hospitals routinely maintain on patients. Medical records typically contain names, street addresses, and various other forms of information on hospital utilization. A hospital that wants to compare the demographic characteristics of its patients with those of neighborhood populations from which the patients are drawn can geocode its medical records using the GBF/DIME procedure. The full range of census geographic codes will be assigned to each record. Thus, for example, the address 4365 Richmond Avenue, appearing on a patient record, will be located in the proper county, MCD or CCD, census tract, ED or block group, and block (if appropriate). Once the geocoding has been completed, hospital utilization patterns can be established for different census areas, and the demographic characteristics of patients and area residents can be compared. The ability to convert systems of administrative records to the same geographic scale as census information is the principal feature of the GBF/DIME procedure.

Apart from the statistical information the Census Bureau produces in conjunction with a decennial census, maps represent one of the most important census products. Census maps are necessary for virtually all uses of small-area census statistics. Demographers must frequently be able to locate specific geographic areas on a map sheet. The Census Bureau produces two different kinds of maps. The first category includes outline maps—maps that identify administrative and statistical area boundaries in relation to other geography. Outline maps do not contain census statistics; they are not intended to convey this type of information. The Census Bureau has developed a number of outline map series for release with the 1980 census.

The second category of census maps includes thematic maps. Behind each thematic map is a "theme" involving one or more census subjects. Unlike outline maps, which merely show boundaries, thematic maps are designed to display statistical information. Thus, for example, a thematic map for household income might display the distribution of median household income across census tracts through the use of color codes to identify tracts in different income categories.

The discussion to this point has focused on census products. The Census Bureau also offers a wide range of services to facilitate the use of census information. Some of these services involve direct assistance to individuals, typically on specific issues, while others involve assistance to groups, frequently in the form of training courses and seminars. In addition to the headquarters office in Suitland, Maryland, the bureau serves the larger community of census users through a network of twelve regional offices located in major cities around the country (see Table 2-4). Beyond this network, one can turn for assistance to a wide range of state and local organizations, most of which provide user services under the auspices of various programs the bureau has chosen to establish over the years. One of the major operations in this area is the State Data Center (SDC) program, a federal-state cooperative effort that seeks to increase and improve public access to census information. Under the SDC program, the Census Bureau furnishes statistical products, training, and consultation services to states, which in turn disseminate the products and provide assistance at the local level. Among the possible range of services, most SDCs can process census summary tape files, handle inquiries for information, and provide consultation, user training, library facilities containing census publications, and technical support for research, planning, and other statistical applications.

Apart from the State Data Center program, the Census Bureau has sponsored the creation of the Clearinghouse of Census Data Services,

TABLE 2-4
Census Bureau Regional Office Locations for Data User Services Assistance

States Covered by Regional Office	*Mailing Address**
Connecticut, Massachusetts, New Hampshire, New York (except New York City area), Maine, Rhode Island, Vermont	441 Stuart Street 10th Floor Boston, MA 02116
New York (city and suburbs), New Jersey (northern)	Federal Office Building Room 37-130 26 Federal Plaza New York, NY 10007
Delaware, District of Columbia, Maryland, New Jersey (southern), Pennsylvania	Green Federal Building Room 9226 600 Arch Street Philadelphia, PA 19106
North Carolina, South Carolina, Virginia, West Virginia	230 S. Tryon Street Suite 800 Charlotte, NC 28202
Alabama, Florida, Georgia, Tennessee	1365 Peachtree Street, NE Room 638 Atlanta, GA 30309
Ohio, Michigan	Federal Building Room 565 231 W. Lafayette Street Detroit, MI 48226
Illinois, Indiana, Kentucky	55 E. Jackson Boulevard Suite 1304 Chicago, IL 60604
Iowa, Kansas, Minnesota, Missouri, Wisconsin	One Gateway Center 4th and State Streets Kansas City, MO 66101
Arkansas, Louisiana, Mississippi, Texas	1100 Commerce Street Room 3C54 Dallas, TX 75242
Arizona, Colorado, Nebraska, New Mexico, Oklahoma, South Dakota, Wyoming	575 Union Boulevard P.O. Box 25207 Denver, CO 80225
California, Hawaii	11777 San Vincente Boulevard 8th Floor Los Angeles, CA 90049
Alaska, Idaho, Montana, Nevada, North Dakota, Oregon, Utah, Washington	915 2nd Avenue Room 312 Seattle, WA 98174

*Inquiries should be directed to the Data User Services Officer at the appropriate regional office.

the Census Depository Library program, the Federal-State Cooperative Program for Population Estimates (FSCPE), and the Federal-State Cooperative Program for Population Projections (FSCPP). Each of these programs has the same general objective as the State Data Center program, to facilitate the use of community statistical resources. The clearinghouse consists basically of public and private organizations listed with the Census Bureau to provide a wide range of data services, notably summary tape processing, user training, computer mapping, and preparation of analytical reports. Clearinghouse organizations are not franchised, established, or supported by the Census Bureau.

The Census Depository Library program is designed to supplement the Government Depository Library System, established by Congress to provide greater public access to federal government documents. What the Census Bureau has done under this program is to designate Census Depository Libraries in areas not served by Government Depository Libraries. The Census Libraries stock basic census reports as well as special publication series selected to meet the needs of library patrons.

The two federal-state cooperative programs, the FSCPE and the FSCPP, were established to promote the development and standardization of demographic estimation and projection methods among states and local areas. States are invited by the bureau to participate in both programs. The governor of each state is asked to designate a program representative, which is typically an agency of state government. States may decline to participate in one or both programs, just as they may choose not to enter into other federal-state cooperative arrangements. Most states that have appointed representatives to the FSCPE and the FSCPP have selected agencies already having some special capacity for population estimation and projection work. The FSCPE/FSCPP agencies sometimes also function as state data centers.

A state that joins both cooperative programs and also establishes a state data center is in a strong position to offer census users a wide range of statistical and technical assistance. The appendix to this volume contains a list of member agencies of the State Data Center program, the Federal-State Cooperative Program for Population Estimates, and the Federal-State Cooperative Program for Population Projections, arranged alphabetically by state.

Census Errors

The statement in the Constitution that the population must be enumerated once every ten years for the purpose of reapportioning

Congress belies the complexity of conducting the census operation. Even if the census were taken simply to count people, the task would still be enormous by modern standards. That more recent censuses also collect a lot of other information only adds to the enormity of the task. While the Census Bureau has taken extraordinary measures to control the quality of census enumeration and, thus, to ensure the accuracy of census results, the findings of the decennial census are known to be subject to error.

Three sources of error combine to temper the accuracy of census statistics.

(1) sampling error
(2) coverage error
(3) content over

The first source is present by design. Information collected on a sample basis is necessarily subject to some margin of error. The overall sampling fraction for the 1980 census is around 20 percent; jurisdictions with a population of less than 2500 were sampled at a rate of 50 percent, and those with a larger population were sampled at roughly 17 percent. When the lowest sampling fraction is sufficient to place one-in-six households in the census sample, the minimum statistical reliability for census results obtained through sampling will be quite good, even for areas the size of smaller census tracts.

Coverage and content errors, unlike those due to sampling, cannot be closely regulated through the careful design of census procedures. Sampling errors, as the statistician would say, "behave in predictable ways," and mathematical models of this "behavior" can be used to determine the best sampling strategy in a particular situation. Unfortunately, coverage and content errors do not have the same desirable statistical properties. Coverage errors are created when persons are simply missed by the census count. Content errors arise generally when persons properly counted give incorrect responses to one or more items on the census questionnaire. Thus, for example, a person aged 63 at the time of the census may unintentionally report a date of birth that implies an age of 67. The reasons for misreporting census items are numerous; one of the most common reasons is inadequate recall.

The Census Bureau has made a concerted effort over the past few decades to evaluate the completeness and accuracy of census results and to publish the findings for the benefit of census users. Bureau evaluations have never reached the point of actually recommending adjustments to reported census counts; the technology of census evaluation has simply not been developed to a degree of refinement that permits "final answers." What the bureau has been able to establish, and with what many demographers consider reasonably good accuracy, is the extent of census coverage and content errors for the national population (U.S. Bureau of the Census, 1974). The methodology is quite complex and contains a number of subjective elements. An examination of the census evaluation procedure is beyond the scope of this volume; nevertheless, we can address the basic question of census coverage.

Establishing the relative coverage error for total population in 1980 is confounded to a serious degree by the apparent presence in reported census counts of persons who have come to be designated "illegal aliens"—persons who are not American citizens and who enter the United States without the proper documents and without official permission. Estimates of the number of persons in this category at the time of the 1980 census range from the thousands to the millions; unfortunately, there is no way of knowing the precise figure. In light of this problem, the Census Bureau has prepared estimates of relative coverage error under alternative assumptions about the number of illegal aliens included in the 1980 census count. Most of these scenarios place the error at one or two percent, an encouraging outcome despite the dilemma.

Once the province of only those demographers and statisticians interested in the quality of census information, completeness of coverage became a highly controversial issue in the 1980 census. A group of local governments mounted a major legal challenge to the accuracy of census results, filing suit in the federal courts to prevent the Census Bureau from releasing census counts suspected of being incorrect. The concern local governments have shown for census coverage reflects an underlying concern for equity in the geographic distribution of political representation and public funds. Census results play a major role in reapportionment and allocation formulas. Consequently, states in which census coverage is not particularly good relative to other areas stand to lose both seats in Congress and federal money for public programs.

The Constitution clearly intends the decennial census to be a complete and accurate enumeration of population, and many feel that it is incumbent upon the Census Bureau to show that a census was conducted in accordance with this intent. Unfortunately, achieving a comprehensive accounting in a nation of more than 220 million people may simply not be possible. The prospect that some amount of coverage error is endemic to the census process raises the question of what constitutes an acceptable standard for census accuracy. Judicial review of the undercount matter must consider this question, as well as others, in the context of broader constitutional issues.

3. CURRENT SURVEYS

The preceding chapter establishes the central role of the decennial census in providing comprehensive demographic information for all levels of geography. Because census results become dated with the passage of time, the Bureau of the Census has begun to devote an increasing share of its resources to postcensal census updates. These updates are designed to bring forward in time basic population and housing information found on the decennial schedule. While current information of this type can be extremely useful, much of the information is produced only for larger geographic areas, notably the four census regions and the nation as a whole. These geographic restrictions reflect, to a great degree, the method of data collections; the household survey has its greatest comparative advantage as a method of data collection in large populations, which do not include places like counties, minor civil divisions, and census tracts. As we have already indicated, estimation techniques provide the only effective vehicle for updating the census at lower levels of geography. Despite their limited applicability to small-area work, current surveys do merit discussion as a source of demographic information.

The Census Bureau relies primarily on two national surveys to update the decennial census portrait—the Current Population Survey and the Annual Housing Survey. The following two sections outline these survey programs.

The Current Population Survey

The Current Population Survey (CPS) is the principal source of current demographic information for the nation between censuses. Conducted by the Census Bureau since 1940, the CPS now includes about 66,000 households each month. This sample is large enough to yield statistically reliable information for the nation as a whole, for regions, and sometimes for larger states and metropolitan areas, but not for smaller geographic areas, such as counties, places, and minor civil divisions. Only through something approaching an enumeration of population can we obtain useful amounts of subject detail for smaller geographic units. The dilemma we face here is a statistical one: Given a sample of fixed size (number of observations), subject detail and geographic detail are substitutable, not complementary. Sample surveys like the CPS have their greatest comparative advantage as a method of data collection in large populations.

The CPS covers a wide range of subjects about the population, many of which also appear on the census schedule. Topics include age, sex, race and ethnicity, marital status and living arrangements, education, fertility, and family income. The Census Bureau also uses the CPS to collect information for other federal agencies on subjects that are covered most effectively through household interviews. Among the applications in this category, the program to provide the U.S. Bureau of Labor Statistics with monthly data on employment and unemployment is certainly one of the best known. The CPS also generates the most comprehensive information available between censuses on the demographic characteristics of the labor force. This information includes both basic demographic characteristics and those specifically related to labor force participation, such as occupational category and industrial affiliation.

Other applications of the CPS are numerous. Career planning and placement groups use CPS results to assess employment opportunities, particularly changes that seem to be taking place in different lines of work. Real estate relocation firms can examine CPS migration statistics to understand better the geographic preferences of people who move. Educational planners use CPS findings to study public and private school enrollment trends. Finally, the CPS is an important source of information for those federal agencies that must monitor some of the largest domestic assistance programs, most notably income maintenance, old-age benefits, and benefits for veterans.

CPS statistics are available from the Census Bureau in several different forms. One is a collection of publication series that contain occasional reports on subjects the CPS covers. The series in this collection with the broadest demographic scope is series P-20, *Population Characteristics.* Series P-20 yields about 12-15 reports annually, many dealing with such recurring topics as school enrollment, fertility, geographic mobility, and voting patterns. CPS statistics are also available on computer tape in the form of the Annual Demographic File, a tabulation of individual CPS records conceptually similar to the Public-Use Microdata Samples from the decennial census. In addition to CPS statistics available from the Census Bureau, other federal agencies that draw upon the CPS for information also release reports from time to time.

The Annual Housing Survey

To complement the population information derived from the CPS, and to provide a basis for updating some of the housing results from the decennial census, the Census Bureau inaugurated the Annual Housing Survey (AHS). The bureau conducts this survey for the U.S. Department of Housing and Urban Development (HUD). The AHS actually consists of two separate samples. One is a national sample of approximately 70,000 housing units. The other is a metropolitan sample that covers about 105,000 units distributed systematically across 20 SMSAs. The particular group of SMSAs in the metropolitan sample is modified annually so that 60 different SMSAs can be surveyed in a four-year cycle. Current revisions to the SMSA sample point to expanded metropolitan coverage over the decade of the 1980s.

Reports from the AHS are issued jointly by the Census Bureau and HUD. There are presently two publication series. Statistics from the national sample are released in six reports that comprise Series H-150. The six reports cover (1) general housing characteristics, (2) indicators of housing and neighborhood quality, (3) financial characteristics of the housing inventory, (4) housing characteristics of recent movers, (5) urban and rural housing characteristics, and (6) financial characteristics by indicators of housing and neighborhood quality. Statistical tabulations are presented for the nation as a whole, the four census regions, the aggregate of all SMSAs (distinguishing between the central city and the SMSA balance), and the aggregate of all areas outside SMSAs. Statistics from the metropolitan sample are released in groups of reports that comprise Series H-170. Each group pertains to one of the sample SMSAs. The topical coverage of Series H-170 is similar to that of Series H-150, but the SMSA series does not include the report on urban and rural housing characteristics.

4. VITAL STATISTICS

A cooperative system among states, local areas, and the federal government has long been established in relation to vital statistics. The National Vital Registration System is a well-organized confederation of some 55 state and local registration areas. The system includes the registration programs of the 50 states, the District of Columbia, New York City, Guam, Puerto Rico, and the Virgin Islands; New York City operates a program independent of New York State. Each program is the product of state or local legislation and conforms to general specifications set forth by Congress in the Model State Vital Statistics Laws (as amended). These specifications are intended to provide guidance to states and local areas in the design and operation of their vital registration programs. Guidelines for content, methods, procedures, and standards foster uniformity among the registration areas.

Registration Programs

The United States registers the occurrence of five vital events—birth, death, fetal death (stillbirth), marriage, and divorce. The data collection programs that record information on each of these events are technically separate operations, but the registration process in each case is generally the same.

Persons responsible for reporting vital events (e.g., physician, hospital administrators, funeral directors, ministers, court clerks) initiate the process by completing appropriate registration certificates. A certificate is filed for each registrable vital event in the jurisdiction where the event occurs. These certificates are then sent to the local registration office, where officials verify the completeness and accuracy of the information. The next stop is the state office of vital statistics, which serves as a central certificate collection point, as well as a vital records archive. State offices perform a number of important functions, not the least of which is to maintain official copies of each birth, death, fetal death, marriage and divorce certificate.

The last stop in the registration process is the National Center for Health Statistics (NCHS). An agency of the United States Public Health Survey, NCHS is charged by Congress with the administration of the National Vital Registration System. The certificates NCHS receives from state offices are used to prepare and publish vital statistics for the nation as a whole and for various state and local areas. NCHS also conducts extensive research involving administrative, technical, and legal aspects of vital registration, and maintains a continuing technical assistance program to improve the quality and usefulness of vital statistics.

While the National Vital Registration System provides for the registration of five vital events, not all events are registered in all states and local areas. Only the birth, death, and fetal death programs cover all 55 registration jurisdictions. The marriage program now covers about 80 percent of these areas, and the divorce program covers about 60 percent. Jurisdictions are added to the marriage and divorce programs when they choose to apply and can meet certain administrative and technical criteria.

The various vital registration programs have been operating for differing periods of time. The death registration program was begun officially in 1880, when the Census Bureau established a national "registration area" for deaths. Another registration area—this one for births—came into existence in 1915. The birth and death programs did not cover all existing jurisdictions until 1933. The evolution of the fetal death program parallels the growth of the registration program for births. The marriage and divorce programs are much more recent. The marriage registration area was formally established in 1957, and the divorce registration area was initiated a year later. The varying durations of these programs will affect the availability of vital statistics for historical periods.

Statistical Sources

Applied demographic analysis frequently involves the use of vital statistics. In particular, birth and death statistics play an important role in estimating and projecting population. The next two chapters of this volume contain illustrations of fundamental techniques for demographic estimation that rely heavily on birth and death statistics for local areas. Applied demographers who need vital statistics have several sources to which they can turn. One of the most popular sources is the report series, *Vital Statistics of the United States*, published annually in several volumes by NCHS. Available from basically the same group of agencies and organizations that maintain collections of census documents, these reports present detailed summary tabulations for births, deaths, fetal deaths, marriages, and divorces. Many of these tabulations are classified by selected demographic characteristics; births, for example, are reported by characteristics of the mother and the child. Geographic coverage tends to follow major administrative and statistical boundaries—states, counties, metropolitan areas, and cities. Vital statistics compiled by NCHS also are available on computer tape.

Applied demographers who need information for the most current time period may also turn to the local agencies and state offices that collect and process vital records. Most of these operations maintain summary tabulations with only a month or two delay for vital events registered in their jurisdictions. These tabulations typically consist just of counts for different geographic areas and are based on certificates filed to date. (Our appendix presents a current list of state vital statistics offices.)

Applied demographers who turn to state and local sources for up-to-the-minute vital statistics are cautioned on an important technical matter involving their casual use. Information of this type routinely available from local agencies and state offices is very likely to be classified by "place of occurrence." The other classification scheme commonly used is "place of residence." Tabulations by place of occurrence assign vital events to the geographic areas where they actually occurred. Tabulations by place of residence, however, assign vital events to the areas that represent the "usual residence" of the persons involved. To the extent that vital events would not be assigned to the same geographic area under occurrence and residence definitions, the number of vital events for a particular area in each case may not be the same.

Consider the number of deaths reported for Wilmington, Delaware, in a certain year. If the reporting basis is place of occurrence, then what we have is the number of persons who died in the city, regardless of where they were actually maintaining their usual residence at the time of death. If the reporting basis is place of residence, however, then what we have is the number of "usual" residents of Wilmington who died during the course of the year, regardless of where they happened to be at the time of their death.

Occurrence and residence numbers do not have to be different, but they usually are, and the difference can be substantial. While both place of occurrence and place of residence are useful classifications, most applied demographic work requires the residence definition, if only because other forms of demographic information, notably the decennial census, are reported on a residence basis.

5. ESTIMATING TOTAL POPULATION

The preceding three chapters have covered major sources of demographic data. The reader should now be familiar with data sources for census years for both large and small geographic areas, as well as sources for noncensus years for larger areas. The remaining element in the matrix of data sources from Chapter 1 is the estimation of population for smaller geographic areas in noncensus years. Addressing this element brings us, for the first time, to the methodological side of the field.

This chapter concerns techniques suitable for estimating total population. The three techniques presented are

(1) mathematical extrapolation;

(2) housing unit procedure; and

(3) vital rates procedure.

These techniques are among the most elementary. The final section of this chapter describes quite succinctly some of the more sophisticated methods that applied demographers have developed to estimate total population.

Each section in this chapter describes a particular technique, its data requirements, and the difficulties inherent in developing reliable estimates. The basic format includes a step-by-step illustration of the application of the method, showing the precise computational procedure required. These examples have all been prepared to produce an estimate of the total resident population of Harris County, Texas (location of the city of Houston) on July 1,1982. Our choice of a single area to serve as an illustration should lend more realism to the exercises since, in practice, demographers typically prepare estimates for an area using as many different techniques as possible. The accuracy of an estimate is improved when the results of two or more estimation techniques, based on independent data sources, are averaged (Cavanaugh, 1981). In addition to improved accuracy, the average of several independent estimates of total population can also serve as a "control" total for estimates of demographic detail—a principle we examine in the next chapter.

In preface to this (and the following) chapter, our presentation of estimates for Harris County is designed to be illustrative, not definitive. Our goal here is to show the reader how to prepare estimates of population using various techniques, not to produce estimates of the population of Harris County.

Mathematical Extrapolation

This section describes a basic mathematical procedure for estimating total population. Mathematical methods are quite popular because they are computationally simple and require only the type of data that tend to be routinely available. Unfortunately, mathematical methods ignore the component processes that govern population change. Instead of making explicit allowance for fertility, mortality, and migration, the mathematical method simply lumps these components together in a single measure of demographic change—the average annual growth rate. This approach has the effect of treating population as a numerical aggregate whose change over time can be summarized by a strict mathematical formula.

The time, effort, and cost associated with the use of mathematical methods is usually so minimal that it is easy to forget about their accuracy. As a general rule, mathematical estimates of total population tend to be more accurate (1) the closer the estimate date is to the most recent census and (2) the more stable the patterns of demographic change are for the study area. Thus, for example, using 1970-1980 as a reference period to estimate the average annual rate of population change, a postcensal estimate for 1981 is likely to be more accurate than one for 1987. But, if the rate of growth for the study area is quite stable and well represented by the average rate over the decade, then the difference in accuracy between the 1981 and 1987 estimates may not be that great. Most applications of mathematical procedures involve estimates that postdate a census by only a year or two. Beyond this point, it is advisable to use a more refined estimation technique, such as the housing unit method or the vital rates method.

To illustrate the mathematical procedure for estimating total population, we will prepare an estimate of the total resident population of Harris County, Texas, on July 1, 1982. On line 1 of Table 5-1 we enter the population of Harris County in the 1970 census (1,741,912). On line 2 we enter the corresponding figure from the 1980 census (2,409,547). The period from 1970 to 1980 gives us a reference period for which we can compute an average annual rate of growth. The reference period typically is the period between the two most recent censuses. To compute the average annual growth rate, we first compute the ratio of the 1980 census count to the 1970 count, we then take the *natural* logarithm of this ratio, and finally we divide the logarithm by the length of the time interval (measured in years) between the two censuses.

This series of calculations is shown on lines 3-5 of Table 5-1. Having the average annual growth rate for the study area, we now are in a position to compute the population estimate. On line 6 we enter the elapsed time is 27 months, or 2.25 years. On line 7 we enter the product to estimate, measured in years and fractions of years. The date of the 1980 census is April 1, 1980. The date of the estimate is July 1, 1982. The elapsed time is 27 months, or 2.25 years. on line 7 we enter the product of the elapsed-time figure and the average annual growth rate (0.0730 = 2.25 × 0.0325). On line 8 we enter a number that equals the base of the

TABLE 5-1

Estimating Total Resident Population Using Mathematical Procedures

Study Area: Harris County, Texas

Date of Estimate: July 1, 1982

1. Total resident population from *next most recent* census.	1,741,912
2. Total resident population from *most recent* census.	2,409,547
3. Ratio of *most recent* to *next most recent* census count (line 2/line 1).	1.3833
4. Natural logarithm of line 3.	0.3245
5. Average annual growth rate (line 4/10).	0.0325
6. Elapsed time between most recent census date and date of the estimate—measured in years and fractions of years.	2.25
7. Product of average annual growth rate and elapsed time beyond most recent census (line 5 × line 6).	0.0730
8. Exponential of line 7 using base of natural logarithms.	1.0757
9. Population estimate (line 8 × line 2).	2,592,030

natural logarithms raised to the power of the product we have just computed. The result of this operation is 1.0757 (= $e^{0.0730}$, where e is the base of the natural logarithms).

To complete the estimation procedure, we enter the product of the exponential (line 8) and the most recent (1980) census count (line 2) on line 9. The figure on line 9 (2,592,030) is the estimated total resident population of Harris County on July 1, 1982. What we have done to obtain this estimate is to carry the 1980 census count forward in time 27 months (2.25 years) on the assumption that the average annual growth rate for Harris County between 1970 and 1980 remains unchanged. The procedure we have used here sometimes is called extrapolation; we are extrapolating the 1970-1980 growth trend for Harris County beyond 1980. The figure on line 8, which we have called an exponential, might be termed more appropriately a "growth multiplier." It represents the relative increase in the population of Harris County that must occur between April 1, 1980 and July 1, 1982 if the population is to continue growing at the 1970-1980 average annual rate. The figure on line 8 (1.0757) means that the population of Harris County will increase by 7.6 percent between April 1, 1980 and July 1, 1982, if the average annual rate of change is 3.25 percent.

Housing Unit Procedure

This section describes the housing unit procedure for estimating total population. The housing unit procedure is much more dependent than other methods upon the user's ability to uncover and employ the best data available. There are more potential problems with source, type, and accuracy of data in the application of the housing unit procedure than in the application of other methods described in this volume. For this reason we will devote considerable attention to different sources of housing information, pointing out some of the pitfalls that await the unsuspecting analyst. The next four subsections describe possible data sources and general approaches to the various elements needed to compute a housing unit estimate of population. The fifth subsection presents the step-by-step computational procedure, again using Harris County as an illustration.

The total population residing in the study area (the geographic area for which an estimate is to be prepared) can be divided into two groups: the household population and the population in group quarters. When developing housing unit estimates, it is useful to work separately with these two groups.

1. Estimating group-quarters population. The group-quarters population is generally much smaller than the household population and typically consists of persons who are institutionalized, such as inmates of a prison or patients in a nursing home, and persons who live in places like college dormitories, military barracks, and halfway houses. We will need a count of the number of residents of each group-quarters facility in the study area on or about the date of the population estimate. Unless this information is routinely available, the data will have to be collected through inquiries. We recommend starting with institutions, such as prisons and health facilities, for they are obvious sources of group-quarters population, and in many communities they account for a significant proportion of the group-quarters total. Remember that each institution should be located within the boundaries of the study area. Census Bureau regional offices (see Table 2-4) can provide information on boundary locations, as well as determine whether a particular facility qualifies as a "group-quarters institution" under Census Bureau rules.

The noninstitutional group-quarters population usually presents a greater problem. In many communities the major component of this population can be found in college dormitories or military barracks. But this category also includes persons living in places like halfway houses, boarding houses, and communes, and it is sometimes difficult to know just how many persons are involved. Beyond the more obvious noninstitutional group quarters, such as dormitories and barracks, the Census Bureau generally limits the category to living quarters occupied by at least ten persons not related to the person who owns or rents the quarters. It is best to begin estimating the size of the noninstitutional group-quarters population by contacting all colleges and universities and military installations within the boundaries of the study area. If they have dormitories or barracks, then it is necessary to determine how many persons were quartered on or about the date of the population estimate. As far as halfway houses, boarding houses, and communes are concerned, it will probably be necessary to hazard a guess. Fortunately, guessing may not be all that bad, since the population involved is typically quite small.

If trying to contact group-quarters facilities does not yield satisfactory results, then the next best approach is to consult the 1980 census or a more recent special census. The 1980 census printed reports contain information on both the institutional and noninstitutional group-quarters population. Similar information will have been published for any more recent special census; one can simply call the nearest Census Bureau regional office (Table 2-4) for further information.[2] While census figures become dated with the passage of time, not all census figures become useless with age.

The population living in households, as opposed to group quarters, typically accounts for 90 to 95 percent of the residents of an area. Estimating the household population involves the separate estimation of three components: (1) the number of housing units, (2) the vacancy rate, and (3) the average number of persons per household. The logic of this approach is straightforward. Multiplying the number of housing units by the occupancy rate (one minus the vacancy rate) yields the number of occupied units. Multiplying the number of occupied units by the average number of persons per household yields the household population.

2. Estimating housing units. There are several sources of information for housing unit estimation. The three most common sources are (1) building permits, (2) certificates of occupancy, and (3) utility records. Other sources include sewerage connections (septic counts), post office addressing records, tax assessor records, and newspaper deliveries. For various reasons, such sources do not provide as reliable an indication of the number of housing units in place on a given date. Building permits (authorization to begin construction) are issued by most counties and municipalities. The number of permits issued in an area can usually be obtained from local building officials. If estimates are being prepared for several areas, it will be easier to obtain data on permits from a central source, such as a state statistical abstract, or the Census Bureau's monthly report, "Housing Units Authorized by Building Permits and Public Contracts" (*Current Construction Reports, Series C-40*].

When using building permits to estimate households, it is necessary to have a complete count of housing units on some previous date. An obvious choice is the number reported in the 1980 Census or a more recent special census. To this figure add the number of residential building permits issued between April 1, 1980 (or the date of a more recent special census) and the date of the estimate. Then subtract the number of residential demolitions (units torn down) during the same period. Finally, again for the same period, make an adjustment for the net number of residential conversions, the difference between units converted from commercial and industrial uses to residential use and units converted from residential use to commercial and industrial uses. The result is an estimate of the number of housing units in place on the date of the population estimate.

There are several problems with the use of building permits and demolition records for household estimation. First, not all residential permits refer to housing units. Some refer to garages, storage sheds, swimming pools, and additions to existing structures. In principle, these permits should be removed from the total, but such an adjustment is not always easy. Second, the fact that a permit has been issued for a residence does not necessarily mean that the unit has been built (or ever will be). During adverse economic conditions, in particular, units are sometimes completed a number of months or years after building permits have been issued. Third, in some situations where a multiunit structure is being torn down, the building inspector may record the demolition of the structure rather than the actual number of units. Such an occurrence is common in areas in which it is difficult to know how many separate living quarters are actually located in a building. These three factors can combine to make the household estimate based on building permits and demolition records an overestimate of the number of units actually in place; the final population estimate also will be inflated as a consequence.

The use of certificates of occupancy to estimate housing units tends to overcome at least one of the problems with building permits. We have noted that there can be a lag between the issuance of a permit and the completion of the unit, and furthermore, the lag can be substantial under certain conditions. Using certificates of occupancy will minimize this problem, because a certificate is typically issued only after a unit has been completed and is deemed ready for occupancy. Where possible, we recommend the use of certificates of occupancy rather than building permits. Certificates of occupancy, though, are not as widely available as building permits and cannot be obtained from centralized sources.

In many communities the best source of information on the number of housing units in place at a given point in time is the administrative record system of public utilities. This system associates each housing unit with an electric meter and records the addition of new units (meter connects) and the departure of old ones (meter disconnects). Moreover, a typical system can distinguish occupied units with active meters from vacant units with inactive meters. The only real limitation to the system is master-metering. In some areas a number of multiunit dwellings (apartments) still operate with only one meter in each building; the living units are not individually metered. Thus, without actually visiting these places it is difficult to know just how many separate living quarters a structure contains. Fortunately, visiting apartment buildings with master meters is not a difficult task in smaller communities, and the utility company can readily identify the buildings in question. All that one needs to do is to count the number of separate living quarters (apartments) in each master-metered building. The utility company can then supply the total number of single-meter connects. Adding this figure to the number of units counted in master-metered structures gives what will usually be a very good estimate of the number of housing units in place on a certain date.

We should caution at this point about geographic coding. Whether one uses building permits, certificates of occupancy, or utility records to estimate housing units, the information must be restricted to the boundaries of the study area. With this restriction in mind it is easy to appreciate why housing-unit estimates developed from post office addressing records are not always reliable. Other limitations aside, there is frequently a difference between the geographic limits of a community and the postal patron service area. Utility records represent the one source of information that is usually most easily coded to specific geographic units. A further advantage of utility records is the ease with which they can be coded to relatively small geographic areas.

To summarize, utility records will generally provide the strongest basis for housing unit estimation, and we recommend their use whenever and wherever possible. Second priority should be given to certificates of occupancy, assuming they can be easily obtained at the local level. Building permits, our third choice, tend to be less reliable sources of information than occupancy certificates. If utility records, as well as building permits or certificates of occupancy, are available, we suggest the preparation of housing unit estimates using all three sources. Each source provides a slightly different perspective on the stock of living quarters.

3. Estimating vacancy rates. The second component of the procedure for the estimation of household population is the vacancy rate. Applying a vacancy rate to a housing unit estimate will yield an estimate of the number of occupied units. Although the information tends to become somewhat dated, the best single source of vacancy rates for many local areas is still the 1980 census; one may also resort to a more recent special census. In many states, staff members from the Federal-State Cooperative Program (FSCP) will also be able to provide useful information on vacancy rates. (The current listing of FSCP agencies is shown in the appendix.) We recommend getting in touch with an FSCP agency if census vacancy rates are to be used. There are certain limitations to these rates, most of them minor (such as units held for occasional use or newly constructed units), and agency staff can provide valuable assistance.

Several other sources of vacancy rate information also are available. Utility records, mentioned in connection with household estimation, can also be used to produce vacancy rates. The records are frequently classified in such a manner that active and inactive meters can be distinguished. Dividing the number of inactive (total minus active) meters by the total number of meters yields an estimate of the vacancy rate for metered units. An allowance must be made, of course, for master-metered units; the nature of this allowance was discussed above. Assuming the utility records cover housing units only within the boundaries of the study area, the ratio of inactive meters to total meters should give a fairly good indication of current vacancy conditions. If utility records can be used to estimate housing units, then they should also be used to estimate vacancy rates.

Another source of vacancy rate information is the small-scale household survey. If there is a college or university in the area, it might be a good idea to inquire whether someone at one of these institutions has conducted a recent household survey generally within community boundaries. Vacant units are normally verified for purposes of survey research, making vacancy rate estimation from local surveys a relatively simple task.

The remaining sources of vacancy rate information are more problematic. They include the Annual Housing Survey (AHS), postal vacancy surveys, and real estate multiple-listing services. All have definite limitations. The AHS, discussed in Chapter 3, provides information on vacancy rates only for larger metropolitan areas. While it might be advisable to take a look at the appropriate AHS report, particularly if the study area is in or near one of the AHS sample SMSAs, a survey of this scale can give only a general indication of vacancy conditions for smaller communities. Postal surveys suffer from the problem of jurisdictional correspondence. Almost any city and its postal service area are quite different territories. Similar problems arise with vacancy estimates derived from multiple-listing services. Furthermore, this source will give only the number of vacant units; the total number of housing units must be found elsewhere. It may also be difficult to obtain multiple-listing information; many services impose strict limitations on distribution. As a general rule, we recommend avoiding postal surveys and multiple-listing services as a source of vacancy information.

4. Estimating average household size. The final component of the procedure for the estimation of household population is average household size. Applying an estimate of average household size to an estimate of occupied housing units yields an estimate of resident household population. The primary source of information on average household size, although one to use with some care, is the decennial census. At this writing, the 1980 census is only several years old, and census measures of household size are still likely to be quite accurate. But just a few years from now this may not be the case. Indeed, during the past decade there have been significant changes in both household size and composition. Lower birth rates, higher divorce rates, and changing patterns of marriage and mortality have combined to reduce the number of persons in a typical household. If these trends continue, even at a markedly slower pace, 1980 census household size figures are likely to become increasingly less accurate as the decade passes.

While discussing factors affecting household size, we should probably mention one factor that is frequently overlooked—the relation between household size and type of housing unit (Smith and Lewis, 1980). Larger households tend to be found in single-family homes, while smaller households, including many persons living alone, tend to be found in multiunit dwellings, typically apartments. Consequently, if the mix of housing units in the study area has changed significantly during recent years (comparing successive censuses will give a good indication), then this change probably has produced a corresponding change in overall household size. Just how large the effect might be is difficult to know, but the correlation between housing mix and household size is unmistakable. We mention this relation because it is worth noting in communities where recent residential construction has radically altered the single-family composition of housing units. When the problem exists, one must approach the estimation of average household size in noncensus years with greater care; less emphasis should be placed on census results that are more remote in time.

Another possible source of information is the local household survey. A general-purpose community survey of the type conducted periodically by many colleges and universities can be used not only to estimate vacancy rates, as we have previously indicated, but it can also be used to estimate average household size. The number of persons who usually reside in a household is a common survey question. Estimating average household size from a local survey is a simple task.

Other sources of information on household size include special censuses and the Current Population Survey (CPS). If a special census has been conducted in the study area since the most recent decennial census, the special tabulations probably will contain household summaries. While a special census conducted in 1981 is not likely to show much change (if any at all) in average household size over the 1980 census, one conducted in 1985, for example, might show substantial change. The CPS, mentioned in Chapter 3, also produces survey estimates of average household size. Unfortunately, these estimates continue to be available only for the nation as a whole and for larger regions, states, and cities. While a survey of this scale can give only a general indication of household size in smaller communities, it does provide useful information on recent patterns of household change. The following table presents household sizes for the nation as a whole, and for the four census regions, reported in the 1970 and 1980 censuses and the 1982 CPS (the most recent CPS for which data are available):

AVERAGE HOUSEHOLD SIZE

Source	*United States*	*Northeast Region*	*Northcentral Region*	*South Region*	*West Region*
1970 Census	3.14	3.10	3.20	3.17	3.04
1980 Census	2.75	2.80	2.77	2.79	2.67
1982 CPS	2.72	2.77	2.74	2.76	2.64

We present this information for two reasons: (1) to emphasize just how much household size has declined over the past decade, and (2) to indicate that the decline we have observed nationally has not been concentrated in any one part of the country. These data can also be used to adjust local figures as reported in the most recent census.

We should caution the use of regional CPS figures to represent household size in a particular community. Just as the regional figures vary about the national average, so will the figures for the many communities in a region vary about the regional average. In short, national and regional estimates rarely summarize local conditions very effectively; but such information can still be useful in the population estimation process. The following subsection contains a procedure we recommend in which a local estimate of average household size is based, in part, on the recent change in household size in the corresponding census region.

5. *Methodology.* The purpose of this subsection is to provide step-by-step instructions for preparing a population estimate using the housing unit method. To illustrate the calculations, we have again chosen Harris County, Texas, and will prepare an estimate of total population for July 1, 1982.

We begin with average household size—the number of persons per household. Since we are making an estimate for 1982, we might feel comfortable relying upon the 1980 census. According to the 1980 census, average household size for Harris County is 2.75. If we had reason to believe that this figure might have changed significantly between 1980 and 1982, then we could prepare an estimate of average household size using the 1982 CPS. Taking this route to illustrate the procedure, we first enter the 1980 census household-size figure on line 1 of Table 5-2. On line 2A we enter the 1980 census figure for average household size for the census region in which Texas is located (the South region). One line 2B we enter the 1982 CPS estimate for the South region. Line 3 contains the ratio of line 2B to line 2A—the relative change in regional average household size between 1980 and 1982. On line 4 we enter the product of line 1 and line 3. Multiplying the 1980 census figure for Harris County by the regional change in average household size between 1980 and 1982 yields an estimate of the number of persons per household for Harris County in 1982. If we had decided to use the 1980 census figure for Harris County as the estimate for 1982, rather than preparing a separate estimate, then we simply would have entered this figure directly on line 4. We could also have used a special census figure, if a special census had been conducted since 1980, or a local survey estimate obtained from a college or university.

We now turn to the number of housing units in Harris County. We will use both building permits and utility records to illustrate the estimation procedure. First, on line 5 of Table 5-2 we enter the number

TABLE 5-2
Estimating Total Population Using the Housing Unit Method

Study Area: Harris County, Texas

Date of Estimate: July 1, 1982

Persons Per Household

1. 1980 census persons per household for study area.	2.75
2A. 1980 census persons per household for parent census region of study area (northeast, northcentral, south, or west).	2.79
2B. Current Population Survey persons per household for year of estimate for parent census region of study area.	2.76
3. Ratio of line 2B to line 2A.	0.98
4. Estimated persons per household for date of estimate for study area (line 1 times line 3 OR the 1980 census figure OR a more recent special census or local survey figure).	2.71

Housing Units—Occupancy Certificates/Building Permits

5. Housing unit count—1980 census OR more recent special census.	984,577
6. Number of *residential* certificates of occupancy (building permits) issued since April 1, 1980 or date of a more recent special census.	78,612
7. Number of *residential* demolition permits issued since April 1, 1980 or date of a more recent special census.	1,063
8. Net change in housing units since April 1, 1980 or date of a more recent special census (line 6 minus line 7).	77,549
9. Estimated number of housing units for study area on date of estimate, according to occupancy certificates or building permits (line 5 plus line 8).	1,062,126
10. Number of *residential* utility customers on or about April 1, 1980 or date of a more recent special census.	869,880

Housing Units—Utility Records

11. Number of *residential* utility customers on or about date of estimate.	975,972

Table 5-2 (Continued)

12. Net change in metered housing units since April 1, 1980 or date of a more recent special census (line 11 minus line 10).		106,092
13. Estimated number of housing units for study area on date of estimate, according to utility records (line 5 plus line 12).		1,090,669
Vacancy/Occupancy Rates		
14. Number of *inactive* residential utility meters on or about date of estimate.		126,876
15. Number of residential utility customers on or about date of estimate (same as line 11).		975,972
16. Estimated current vacancy rate (line 14 divided by line 15 OR 1980 census OR figure from more recent special census or local survey).		0.130
17. Estimated current occupancy rate (1.0 minus line 16).		0.870
Population Estimates	*Occupancy Certificates/ Building Permits*	*Utility Records*
18. Estimated number of occupied housing units on date of estimate (line 17 times line 9 for permits; line 17 times line 13 for utility records).	924,050	948,882
19. Estimated household population (line 18 times line 4).	2,504,176	2,571,470
20. Estimated group-quarters population (1980 census OR more recent special census OR independent estimate).	20,179	20,179
21. Estimated total resident population (line 19 plus line 20).	2,524,355	2,591,649

of housing units reported for Harris County in the 1980 census—984,577. If a more recent special census were available, then we should use the housing unit count from this enumeration. On line 6 we enter the number of residential building permits issued in Harris County between April 1, 1980 and March 31, 1982—three months prior to the date of the population estimate. The purpose of this short lag is to allow for the time difference between permit issuance and building completion; we recommend about three months under normal economic conditions. If we were using certificates of occupancy, a time lag would be unnecessary.

Next, on line 7 we enter the number of residential demolition permits issued during the same time period—April 1, 1980 to March 31, 1982. Line 8, the difference between line 6 and line 7, represents the net change in the number of housing units in Harris County since the 1980 census. The data on lines 6 and 7 were obtained from local building reports, available through the Houston Chamber of Commerce. Line 9, the sum of lines 5 and 8, is the estimated number of housing units in Harris County on July 1, 1982. If a special census figure had been used on line 5, the number of building permits/occupancy certificates (line 6) and demolition permits (line 7) would have been measured from the date of the special enumeration.

The estimation of housing units from utility records is mechanically similar to the certificate-of-occupancy procedure. We start from the same base—the 1980 census housing-unit count (line 5). On line 10 we enter the number of residential utility customers (active meters) in Harris County on or about April 1, 1980. On line 11 we enter the corresponding figure for July 1, 1982. Both figures were obtained from the local utility company. The figure on line 12, the difference between lines 10 and 11, measures the net change in active meters (metered housing units) since the 1980 census. Adding this difference to the 1980 census housing unit count (line 5) yields an estimate of the number of housing units in place in Harris County on July 1, 1982. In estimating the size of the housing stock from utility records, we again want to emphasize three points: (1) The area for which the utility provides data should match exactly the boundaries of the study area; (2) the utility records should cover only residential meters; and (3) an adjustment should be made for master-metered units.

The final parameter we must estimate is the vacancy/occupancy rate. According to the 1980 census, the overall residential vacancy rate for Harris County is 11.65 percent. If we decide to use the census vacancy rate as the 1981 estimate, we would simply enter 0.1165 on line 16 and then compute the occupancy rate (0.8835) on line 17. If, however, we had reason to believe that the Harris County vacancy rate had changed significantly between 1980 and 1982, then we could prepare a separate estimate. In this case our options would include (1) a more recent special census, (2) a local household survey for Harris County containing vacancy rate information, or (3) the same utility records used to estimate the number of housing units. To illustrate an alternative approach, we have chosen the third option—a utility-record estimate of the vacancy rate. On line 14 we enter the number of inactive residential utility meters on or about July 1, 1982. On line 15 we enter the total number of residential utility customers (from line 11). Dividing line 14 by line 15 yields an estimate of the Harris County vacancy rate (line 16). Subtracting this figure from 1.0 yields a corresponding estimate of the occupancy rate (line 17). Note that the estimated 1982 vacancy rate is really not that different from the 1980 census figure of 11.65 percent.

We are now ready to assemble the final population estimate. On line 18 we compute the estimated number of occupied housing units in Harris County on July 1, 1982, using both building permits and utility records. In the former case the estimated number is 924,050 (line 17 times line 9). In the latter the estimate is 948,882 (line 17 times line 13). We now multiply the number of occupied housing units (line 18) by average household size (line 4) to obtain the estimated household population (line 19). The household populations using building permits and utility records are 2,504,176 and 2,571,470, respectively. According to the 1980 census, the population in group-quarters (nonhousehold population) for Harris County is 20,179. Since the date of the population estimate (1982) is only two years after the census, it is highly unlikely that the group-quarters figure has changed significantly (or at all). In any event, the figure is such a small proportion of total population (less than one percent) that the cost of assuming no change in the group-quarters category between 1980 and 1982 is almost certainly considerably less than the cost of collecting the data needed to develop an independent 1982 estimate. Consequently, we have chosen to use the 1980 census group-quarters count in the estimation process. Had this population been larger, or subject to frequent change, it would have been advisable to follow the procedure suggested in the subsection on estimating group-quarters population. Adding the group-quarters figure (line 20) to the estimated household population (line 19) yields an estimate of the total resident population of Harris County on July 1, 1982. The estimates using building permits and utility records (each shown on line 21 are 2,524,355 and 2,591,649.

Vital Rates Procedure

Unlike the housing unit method, the vital rates approach has modest data requirements; most of the data needed can be found in widely available publications. The vital rates method also is simple mechanically. One must locate the following information to use the vital rates procedure:

(1) the number of births and deaths for the current (estimation) year for the study area;

(2) the number of births and deaths for the same area for the year of the most recent census;

(3) the population count of the study area in the most recent census;

(4) the number of births and deaths for a larger area, which we will call the "reference area," that includes the study area as a part, for both the current year and the most recent census year. As a general rule, we suggest using the next higher level of geography as a reference area, whenever possible. Thus a city might serve as the reference area for a municipal health district or school attendance zone, a county might serve as a reference for a city, a state for a county, and so on;

(5) the population of the reference area for both the current year and the most recent census year.

Information on the population of the study area at the time of the previous census, and of the reference area for both the current and census years, can be obtained from either a Federal-State Cooperative Program agency (see appendix) or the Census Bureau. Generally, figures on births and deaths for any state may be obtained from the vital statistics office of the state health department. (The appendix also gives addresses and telephone numbers for these offices.) Vital statistics are always available for counties, nearly always for cities, and occasionally for subcity and subcounty areas such as census tracts and minor civil divisions. Local health departments can sometimes provide birth and death information in summary form.

The premise of the vital rates method is that the observed change (from census year to estimation year) in birth or death rates for the reference area will occur to roughly the same degree for the study area—demographic change at lower levels of geography mirrors change at higher levels. The actual estimation procedure is based on the definition of an annual vital rate:

$$VR = VE/POP$$

where VR is the vital rate, VE is the number of vital events occurring in a given (calendar) year, and POP is the midyear population (or a figure, such as a census count, generally in the vicinity of July 1). Solving this equation for POP yields the ratio VE/VR. Thus, if we know the number of vital events in the current year and can estimate the corresponding vital rate directly without making the calculation in equation 1, then we are clearly in a position to estimate current population. The vital rate VR that we use in this procedure can be either a birth rate or a death rate. To minimize the potential for error, we suggest preparing an estimate of population for both rates and then averaging the results; indeed, we will take this approach in our illustration of the method of Harris County.

We should caution the use of an *annual* vital rate to estimate population for smaller areas. When an area contains generally fewer than 25,000 persons, we recommend basing the vital rates analysis on several years of vital events, whenever possible. Thus, for example, a 1982 estimate of population might be based on an annual average of vital events for the period 1980-1982, instead of just 1982; the "averaging period" does not have to be centered on the estimation year but should include it. The need to average is the result of random fluctuation in the number of vital events from year to year that can distort the representativeness of vital rates computed for any one year. The vital rates method we describe in Table 5-3 is identical to the procedure we propose for smaller areas, once an *average* annual number of vital events has been obtained.

The vital rates method is limited by the need to assume a fixed relation between reference-area and study-area vital rates. The true relation may vary over time for a number of reasons, most notably because the basic demographic structure of the two areas changes disproportionately. Birth and death rates are quite sensitive to change in the age-sex-race composition of population, particularly in smaller geographic areas. Behavioral factors underlying fertility and mortality also may affect reference-area and study-area vital rates to different degrees over time. As will all demographic estimation methods, the time interval between the base [census] year and the year of the estimate tends to influence the accuracy of the result. Generally, the longer the time interval, the less plausible the assumption that any two sets of vital rates bear a fixed relation to one another and, thus, the more likely the population estimate is subject to measurable error.

The example we will present to illustrate the vital rates method involves, once again, Harris County, Texas. The estimation year is 1982, the estimate date is July 1, and the reference area we have chosen is the entire state of Texas. From the results of the 1980 census, we know the population of the study area on the census date is 2,409,547, and the population of the reference area is 14,229.191. From current estimates

TABLE 5-3
Estimating Total Population Using the Vital Rates Method

Study Area: Harris County, Texas

Date of Estimate: July 1, 1982

1.	Number of births for reference area for year of most recent census. (a)	268,717
2.	Birth rate for reference area for year of the most recent census.	0.01888
	A. Census count for reference area: 14,229,191 (b)	
	B. Number of births (line 1): 268,717 (a)	
	C. Birth rate (2B/2A): 0.01888	
3.	Number of births for study area for year of the most recent census. (a)	50,427
4.	Birth rate for study area for year of most recent census.	0.02093
	A. Census count for study area: 2,409,547 (b)	
	B. Number of births (line 3): 50,427 (a)	
	C. Birth rate (4B/4A): 0.02093	
5.	Ratio of birth rate in study area to reference area.	1.1086
	A. Birth rate of study area (line 4): 0.02093	
	B. Birth rate of reference area (line 2): 0.01888	
	C. Ratio (5A/5B): 1.1086	
6.	Number of births in reference area for the estimation year. (a)	295,013
7.	Birth rate for reference area for the estimation year.	0.01938
	A. Estimate of population of reference area: 15,221,000 (c)	
	B. Number of births (line 6): 295,013 (a)	
	C. Birth rate (7B/7A): 0.01939	
8.	Birth rate for study area for the estimation year.	0.02149
	A. Birth rate ratio of study area to reference area (line 5): 1.1086	
	B. Reference area current birth rate (line 7): 0.10938	
	C. Estimated study area birth rate (8A × 8B): 0.02149.	
9.	Number of births in study area for the estimation year. (a)	55,722
10.	Estimated population of study area using the birth-rate approach.	2,593,307
	A. Number of births (line 9): 55,722 (a)	
	B. Study-area birth rate (line 8): 0.02149	
	C. Population estimate (10A/10B): 2,593,307	

Table 5-3 (Continued)

11.	Number of deaths for reference area for year of most recent census. (a)	108,586
12.	Death rate for reference area for year of most recent census. A. Census count for reference area: 14,229,191 (b) B. Number of deaths (line 11): 108,586 (a) C. Death rate (12B/12A): 0.00763	.00763
13.	Number of deaths for study area for year of most recent census. (a)	14,849
14.	Death rate for study area for year of most recent census. A. Census count for study area: 2,409,547 (b) B. Number of deaths (line 13): 14,849 (a) C. Death rate (14B/14A): 0.00616	.00616
15.	Ratio of study-area death rate to reference-area rate. A. Death rate of study area (line 14): 0.00616 B. Death rate of reference area (line 12): 0.00763 C. Ratio (15A/15B): 0.80755	0.80755
16.	Number of deaths in reference area for the estimation year. (a)	112,444
17.	Death rate for reference area for estimation year. A. Estimate of population of reference area: 15,221,000 (c) B. Number of deaths (line 16): 112,444 (a) C. Death rate (17B/17A): 0.00739	.00739
18.	Death rate for study area for estimation year. A. Death-rate ratio, study area to reference area (line 15): 0.80755 B. Reference-area current death rate (line 17): 0.00739 C. Estimated study area death rate (18A × 18B): 0.00597	0.00597
19.	Number of deaths in study area for the estimation year. (a)	15,555
20.	Estimated population of study area from death data. A. Number of deaths (line 19): 15,555 B. Study-area death rate (line 18): 0.00597 C. Population estimate (20A/20B): 2,607,399	2,607,399
21.	Average vital rates population estimate. A. Estimate from birth data (line 10): 2,593,307 B. Estimate from death data (line 20): 2,607,399 C: Average (21A plus 21B divided by 2): 2,600,353	2,600,353

SOURCES:
(a) State or local health department.
(b) Bureau of the Census: decennial census results.
(c) Federal-State Cooperative Program agency or Census Bureau.

of population, such as those prepared by the Census Bureau (*Current Population Reports*, Series P-25), we can determine that the population of the reference area on July 1, 1982 had grown to 15,221,000. From annual statistical reports of the Texas Department of Health, we compiled the following information on the annual number of births and deaths for Texas and for Harris County during 1980 and 1982:

	TEXAS		HARRIS COUNTY	
	Births	*Deaths*	*Births*	*Deaths*
1980	268,717	108,586	50,427	14,849
1982	295,013	112,444	55,722	15,555

With all this information in hand, we can compute a 1982 estimate of the population of Harris County using the vital rates method. Table 5-3 presents the computation format, and we will now summarize the procedure.

Line 1 of Table 5-3 is the number of births for the state of Texas, the reference area, during the year of the most recent census (1980). The entry is 268,717. In line 2 we divide the number of births by the 1980 reference-area population (14,229,191) to obtain the Texas birth rate (0.01888). Lines 3 and 4 repeat the birth rate calculation in 1980 for Harris County. Line 5 is the ratio of the computed birth rate for the study area to that of the reference area. The result is 1.1086. Next, in line 6 and 7 we compute the birth rate for the reference area in the estimation year (1982). The result is 0.01939. Now, line 8 we determine the birth of the study area for the estimation year. Since we are assuming a fixed relation from 1980 to 1982 between reference-area and study-area vital rates, this estimate is simply the 1980 birth-rate ratio (1.1086), multiplied by the computed 1982 reference-area birth rate (0.01938). The result is 0.02149. Line 9 is the number of births recorded for residents of the study area during the estimation year. The figure is 55,722. In line 10, we are finally able to compute the population estimate for Harris County. We know from equation 1 that estimated population equals recorded vital events divided by an estimated vital rate. The number of births to residents of Harris County during 1982 is 55,722. The estimated birth rate for the county in this year is 0.02149. Dividing the former by the latter yields the estimated total resident population of Harris County on July 1, 1982. The result is 2,593,307.

Lines 11 to 20 repeat the entire estimation process using deaths and death rates rather than births and birth rates. By completing an identical set of calculations, we arrive at the 1982 population estimate shown on line 20 (2,607,399).

Finally, on line 21 we combine the birth rate and death rate estimates of total population to produce a single figure for the year 1982. The final estimate of population for Harris County is the arithmetic average of the separate estimates using births (2,593,307, from line 10) and deaths (2,607,399, from line 20). The result is 2,600,353.

The issue of group-quarters (nonhousehold) population has not been treated in the discussion of the vital rates method. If the study area has a small group-quarters population, or if there is reason to believe that the population has not changed significantly since the most recent census, then no group-quarters adjustment to the final population estimate is necessary. If such an adjustment appears warranted, however, a simple procedure can be followed. Returning to Table 5-3, in lines 4A and 14A we subtract the census count of persons in group quarters at the time of the most recent census from the total and compute the birth and death rates (lines 4 and 14) only for the non-group-quarters (household) population. Then, after averaging the two population estimates (line 21), we add back the *current* size of the group-quarters population (determined from facility and institutional inquiries and other sources) to obtain a final population estimate for the study area.

The vital rates method may also be employed to estimate the demographic characteristics of a population. In general, this may be accomplished by focusing on those individuals to whom vital events occur. Thus the count of deaths by age of decedent may be used to estimate age structure, or the number of births may be used to estimate the number of women in the childbearing years. Similarly, racial or ethnic composition may be estimated by considering births or deaths classified by the race or ethnicity of the decedent's mother. A simple illustration of such extensions is included in the following chapter.

Final Estimate of the Total Population

Using the three methods presented in this chapter, we have actually produced four estimates of the total population of Harris County, Texas, on July 1, 1982:

- mathematical method—2,592,030
- housing unit method (building permits)—2,524,355
- housing unit method (utility records)—2,591,649
- vital rates method (average)—2,600,353

As we noted at the beginning of the chapter, the overall accuracy of a population estimate usually is increased when the estimate is based on the average of the results of several different procedures. In the case of Harris County, we would recommend averaging three of the four individual results to produce the final population estimate. These results are those from the mathematical extrapolation, housing unit (utility records), and vital rates methods. The three figures are remarkably similar, falling within a range of only 8,700 persons in a population of 2.6 million, a discrepancy of just 0.3 percent. Our final estimate, then is 2,594,677.

Other Methods for Estimating Total Population

Apart from the three more elementary techniques discussed in this chapter, applied demographers have developed several other procedures for estimating total population. These more advanced methods typically have more substantial data requirements and involve more elaborate computational schemes than those introduced here. While limitations of space preclude any extensive discussion of such refined procedures, it seems appropriate to describe briefly several of the more popular ones.

The *regression* (or *ratio-correlation*) method requires one to estimate an equation in which the ratio of the share of total population represented by a given subarea at any two points in time (typically, the two most recent census years) is a function of that subarea's share of several other "coincident" indicators likely to mirror changes in population. Indicators commonly used include vital events, school enrollment, automobile licenses, tax returns, and voter registrations. The regression coefficients are estimated across all subunits included in the larger study area (counties in a state, tracts in a city) and are assumed to remain constant over the period since the most recent census. Postcensal changes in each area's share of each indicator are used to estimate postcensal changes in each area's share of total population. Although the regression method is generally quite accurate, it clearly demands a lot of data and some computational sophistication (Schmitt and Crosetti, 1954; O'Hare, 1976; Pursell, 1970; Rosenberg, 1968; Spar and Martin, 1979).

The *component* method was developed by the Census Bureau to produce separate estimates of the components of population change and, more specifically, net migration (net civilian migration in areas with large military populations). The method yields a migration estimate by comparing actual school enrollment in the estimation year with expected enrollment, the latter equaling school-aged population reported in the most recent decennial census minus postcensal deaths to children of school age. Differences between actual and expected enrollment for the estimation year are attributed to net migration. Net migration of school-aged children are translated into net migration rates for total population on the basis of the ratio of school-aged rate to total net migration rate observed during the most recent intercensal period. The total net migration rate is then applied to the "survived" population in the estimation year (total population in the most recent census, plus postcensal births, minus postcensal deaths), to obtain the total number of net migrants during the postcensal period. Natural increase is computed directly from area vital statistics. On the whole, the component method yields accurate results, although the restrictive assumptions with respect to net migration rates—specifically the assumption of a constant ratio between rates for school-aged and total populations—may present problems in the case in which the postcensal period is longer than just a few years and migration patterns are thought to be less stable. It is difficult for the practitioner without access to unpublished census materials to use this method effectively, due to the application of detailed (by age) migration ratios and population counts for small areas (Shryock and Siegel, 1976: 424-446).

More recent developments in the field of demographic estimation have led to the emergence of the *administrative-records* and *synthetic* methods. Administrative records estimation is made possible by a set of matched federal income tax returns filed by individuals in successive years. By comparing place of residence on consecutive returns, it is possible to measure the net migration of persons (based on the number of tax exemptions) on an annual basis (or longer) for most administrative and statistical units in census geography. While the method offers great potential, its accuracy for small areas is difficult to establish. In addition, confidentiality restrictions preclude the use of the federal tax tabulations by anyone other than Census Bureau personnel (Cavanaugh, 1981).

Synthetic methods are regression based, like ratio-correlation, with the independent variables representing proportions of small-area population falling into mutually exclusive and completely exhaustive classes. Unlike ratio-correlation, however, synthetic coefficients are estimates of the mean value of each of these classes based on census or large-scale survey results. In essence, observed changes in demographic parameters for some large population (like the state of Texas) are assumed to hold equally for smaller (and possibly component) areas (like the city of Houston). Thus baseline compositional differences among small areas determine differences in population growth during the post censal period. These methods can prove quite useful, but their application requires considerable technical expertise (Levy, 1979).

6. ESTIMATING DEMOGRAPHIC CHARACTERISTICS

Business and government planning and reporting requirements involving demographic information for smaller geographic areas can frequently be satisfied simply by estimates of total population. Using one or more of the methods described in Chapter 5, the analyst can readily address the needs of those who just want to know "how many people were living in census tract 123 on July 1, 1982." Many of the domestic assistance programs operated by the federal government require only current estimates of basic demographic aggregates, such as total population, to allocate millions of dollars among states and local areas. A notable example in this category is the general revenue sharing program whose allocation formulas use current estimates of total population and several other basic demographic measures to distribute public funds down to the county level.

The Growing Need for Characteristic Detail

While most planning and reporting requirements continue to involve only estimates of total population, a growing number are beginning to include estimates for various population subgroups. The most commonly used classifiction variables are age, sex, and race/ethnicity. The health planner who wants to summarize rates of hospital (inpatient) utilization for a particular community (health service area) will need estimates of population by age and sex: total population aged 15 and over for medical-surgical beds, female population aged 15 to 44 for obstetric beds, and total population aged 14 and under for pediatric beds. The labor economist who wants to examine local personnel recruitment patterns in light of certain Equal Employment Opportunity (EEO) regulations will need estimates of population by sex and race. The real estate marketing assistant who wants to evaluate the potential demand for a high-rise residential condominium in a large urban area will need local population estimates not only for basic demographic characteristics, but also for important classifications such as marital status, educational attainment, household income, and work experience.

The technology of demographic estimation for small geographic areas is not developed to the point at which applied demographers can easily respond to a wide range of requests for current information on demographic characteristics. While the demand for more and greater characteristic detail clearly exists and continues to grow, the supply has been slow to expand—a situation typical of the evolving interaction of information requirements and information technology. The estimation of demographic characteristics for small geographic areas, such as minor civil divisions and census tracts, requires a richness of data base and strength of methodology that exceed those necessary for the estimation of basic demographic aggregates, such as total population and total households. The problem is conceptually similar to the sample size problem in survey research, where only more observations can provide the information base to support parameter estimation with greater detail at a given level of statistical precision.

Applied demographers have begun to devote more attention to the estimation of characteristic detail for smaller geographic areas. Techniques now exist to produce credible estimates for basic demographic characteristics, notably age, sex, and race/ethnicity. Other techniques, including those for a number of economic and social characteristics, are "under construction"; even if they were now in general use, an account of these techniques would be beyond the scope of this volume. To demonstrate the scale and complexity of effort associated with the estimation of demographic characteristics, as well as the depth of data requirements, we have selected the vital rates procedure for age estimation. The age structure of an area is generally considered one of the most important demographic factors for planning and marketing purposes.

Vital Rates Procedure for Age Estimation

To maintain continuity in our illustrations, we will continue preparing estimates for the population of Harris County, Texas, on July 1, 1982. In Chapter 5 we arrived at a final total population estimate for Harris County that will serve as a "control" total for the methods discussed in this chapter. Once again, we strongly recommend the use of control totals when producing estimates of demographic detail. Our rationale is that methods designed to work effectively with population subgroups cannot always be relied upon to work equally effectively with total population. Thus, for example, a technique focusing on the estimation of age groups may not yield a plausible estimate of total population when the separate age-group estimates are summed. The problem stems from the cumulative effect on total population of errors associated with the estimation of smaller population subgroups. When the objective is an estimate of total population, then the best strategy is to estimate the total directly, as we did in Chapter 5. Procedures of the type we discuss in the present chapter can then be used as a basis for allocating the estimated total to various population categories.

The vital rates procedure for estimating total population (see Chapter 5) can be adapted to estimate population by age groups. To produce population estimates by age, it is necessary to obtain the population distribution in the desired age categories, and data on deaths must be available for the same age groups.

The techniques and assumptions employed to produce age estimates using vital rates procedures are essentially the same as those required to produce estimates of total population. Birth and death rates are computed in the census year for both the reference and study areas, and for the reference area in the estimation year. By assuming that the census-year relation between the reference-area and study-area vital rates applies equally in the estimation year, both current vital rates and current population by age for the study area can be determined. The age-specific vital rates procedures presented here permits the estimation of population by broad age groups. More detailed data on births and deaths by age allow more detailed age estimates of the current study-area population, *but* because deaths by fairly narrow age groups (e.g., one- and five-year groups) are rather volatile from year to year even for large areas, we do not recommend age estimation with substantial detail. Even when births and deaths are averaged over several years to reduce random fluctuation—an approach we discussed in Chapter 5—such fluctuations can be (and usually are) still a problem.

Table 6-1 presents the basic data needed to estimate the age distribution of Harris County on July 1, 1982. Once again, we will use the state of Texas as the reference area.

The vital rates procedure we will be applying to Harris County permits the estimation of the population in age groups 0-14, 15-44 (by sex), 45-64, and 65+. Deaths are used to estimate the population for the two oldest age groups; births are used to estimate the female population aged 15-44; the sex ratio from the most recent census is used to estimate the number of males aged 15-44; and a modified child-woman ratio (to be explained later) is used to estimate the population aged 0-14. Once we have completed the age estimation, we will control the estimated age distribution to the final independent estimate of total population developed in Chapter 5.

The first age group to be estimated for Harris County is the population 65 and over. The procedure begins on line 1 of Table 6-2, where we compute the reference-area (Texas) death rate for persons aged 65+ in 1980 (year of the most recent census). The number of deaths in question (53,594) is divided by the census count 65+ (1,371,161), to produce the rate shown on line 1 (0.03909). Line 2 contains the study-

TABLE 6-1
Population by Age and Vital Events: Texas and Harris County, 1980 and 1982

	State of Texas			
Age	*1980 Population*	*1980 Deaths*	*1982 Population*	*1982 Deaths*
0-14	3,518,939	7,222	3,751,000	5,218
15-44	6,802,481	14,145	7,321,000	13,902
Total female	3,377,700		3,635,000	
45-64	2,536,611	33,625	2,694,000	25,405
65+	1,371,161	53,594	1,455,000	57,919
Total	14,229,191	108,586	15,221,000	112,444

	Harris County		
Age	*1980 Population*	*1980 Deaths*	*1982 Deaths*
0–14	597,509	829	736
15-44	1,268,302	2,269	2,363
Total female	624,566		
45-64	396,655	4,798	5,137
65+	147,081	6,953	7,319
Total	2,409,547	14,849	15,555

	1980 Births	*1982 Births*
State of Texas	268,717	295,013
Harris County	50,427	55,722

area death rate among persons aged 65+ in the census year. Again, deaths (6,953) are divided by population (147,081) to produce the result (0.04727). In line 3 we calculate the ratio of death rates for persons aged 65+ between the study area and reference area in the census year. In line 4 we compute the estimation-year death rate for persons aged 65+ in the reference area. Once again, the number of deaths in the age group (57,919) is divided by the estimated population (1,455,000) to obtain the current age-specific death rate (0.03981). In line 5 we compute the estimated death rate for the study-area population aged 65+. Here,

(text continues page 72)

TABLE 6-2
Estimating Population by Age Using the Vital Rates Method

Study Area: Harris County, Texas

Date of Estimate: July 1, 1982

Estimate of the Number of Persons Aged 65+

1. Death rate for persons 65+ in reference area for year of most recent census. — 0.03909
   A. Population 65+ in reference area: 1,371,161 (a)
   B. Deaths in census year to persons 65+: 53,594 (b)
   C. Age-specific death rate (1B/1A): 0.03909

2. Death rate for persons 65+ in study area for year of most recent census. — 0.04727
   A. Population 65+ in study area: 147,081 (a)
   B. Deaths in census year to persons 65+: 6,953 (b)
   C. Age-specific death rate (2B/2A): 0.04727

3. Ratio of death rates for persons 65+. — 1.20945
   A. Reference-area death rate for persons 65+ (line 1): 0.03909
   B. Study-area 65+ death rate (line 2): 0.04727
   C. Ratio (3B/3A): 1.20945

4. Death rate for persons 65+ in reference area for estimation year. — 0.03981
   A. Population 65+ in reference area: 1,455,000 (c)
   B. Deaths in estimating year to persons 65+: 57,919 (b)
   C: Age-specific death rate (4B/4A): 0.03981

5. Estimated death rate for persons 65+ in study area for estimation year. — 0.04814
   A. 65+ death-rate ratio (line 3): 1.20945
   B. Reference-area 65+ death rate (line 4): 0.03981
   C. Estimated study-area death rate for persons 65+ (5A × 5B): 0.04814

Estimate of the Number of Persons Aged 45-64

6. Estimated population 65+ for study area. — 152,022
   A. Study-area deaths among persons 65+ in estimation year: 7,319 (b)
   B. Estimated 65+ death rate (line 5): 0.04814
   C. Population estimate (6A/6B): 152,022

Table 6-2 (Continued)

7. Death rate for persons 45-64 in reference area for year of most recent census. A. Population 45-64 in reference area: 2,536,611 (a) B. Deaths in census year to persons 45-64: 33,625 (b) C. Age-specific death rate (7B/7A): 0.01326	0.01326
8. Death rate for persons 45-64 in study area for year of most recent census. A. Population 45-64 in study area: 396,655 (a) B. Deaths in census year to persons 45-64: 4,798 (b) C. Age-specific death rate (8B/8A): 0.01210	0.01210
9. Ratio of study-area and reference area death rates for persons 45-64, for year of most recent census. A. Reference-area 45-64 death rate (line 7): 0.01326 B. Study-area 45-64 death rate (line 8): 0.01210 C. Ratio of death rates (9B/9A): 0.91252	0.91252
10. Death rate for persons 45-64 in reference area for estimation year. A. Population 45-64 in reference area: 2,694,000 (c) B. Deaths among persons aged 45-64: 35,405 (b) C. Age-specific death rate (10B/10A): 0.01314	0.01314
11. Estimated death rate for persons 45-64 in study area for estimation year. A. 45-64 death-rate ratio (line 9): 0.91252 B. Reference area 45-64 death rate (line 10): 0.01314 C. Estimated study area 45-64 death rate (11A × 11B): 0.01199	0.01199
12. Estimated population 45-64 for study area. A. Study area deaths to persons 45-64 in estimation year: 5,137 (b) B. Estimated 45-64 death rate (line 11): 0.01199 C. Population estimate (12A/12B): 428,351	428,351
Estimate of the Number of Persons Aged 15-44	
13. Fertility rate for reference area in year of most recent census. A. Female population 15-44: 3,377,700 (a) B. Births in census year: 268,717 (b) C. Fertility rate (13B/13A): 0.07956	0.07956
14. Fertility rate for study area in year of most recent census. A. Female population 15-44: 624,566 (a) B. Births in census year: 50,427 (b) C. Fertility rate (14B/14A): 0.08074	0.08074

(continued)

Table 6-2 (Continued)

15. Fertility-rate ratio in census year. 1.01487

    A. Reference-area fertility rate (line 13): 0.07956
    B. Study-area fertility rate (line 14): 0.08074
    C. Fertility-rate ratio (15B/15A): 1.01487

16. Fertility rate for reference area in estimation year. 0.08116

    A. Female population aged 15-44: 3,635,000 (c)
    B. Births in estimating year: 295,013 (b)
    C. Fertility rate (16B/16A): 0.08116

17. Estimated fertility rate for study area in estimation year. 0.08237

    A. Fertility-rate ratio (line 15): 1.01487
    B. Reference-area fertility rate (line 16): 0.08116
    C. Estimated study-area fertility rate (17A × 17B): 0.08237

18. Estimated female population aged 15-44 for study area. 676,518

    A. Study-area births: 55,722 (b)
    B. Estimated fertility rate (line 17): 0.08237
    C. Population estimate (18A/18B): 676,518

19. Sex ratio (number of males per female) of persons 15-44 for study area in year of most recent census. 1.03069

    A. Male population 15-44: 643,736 (a)
    B. Female population 15-44: 624,566 (a)
    C. Sex ratio (19A/19B): 1.03069

20. Estimated male population aged 15-44 for study area. 697,283

    A. Estimated female population 15-44 (line 18): 676,518
    B. Sex ratio (line 19): 1.03069
    C. Population estimate (20A × 20B): 697,283

21. Estimated total population aged 15-44 for study area. 1,373,801

    A. Estimated female population 15-44 (line 18): 676,518
    B. Estimated male population 15-44 (line 20): 697,283
    C. Population estimate (21A + 21B): 1,373,801

Estimate of the Number of Persons Aged 0-14

22. Child-woman ratio (CWR) for reference area in year of most recent census. 1.04181

    A. Population aged 0-14: 3,518,938 (a)
    B. Female population aged 15-44: 3,377,700 (a)
    C. Child-woman ratio (22A/22B): 1.04181

Table 6-2 (Continued)

23. Child-woman ratio for study area in the year of most recent census. — 0.95668
    A. Population aged 0-14: 597,509 (a)
    B. Female population aged 15-44: 624,566 (a)
    C. Child-woman ratio (23A/23B): 0.95668

24. Child-woman ratio for study area relative to reference area in year of most recent census. — 0.91828
    A. Reference-area CWR (line 22): 1.04181
    B. Study-area CWR (line 23): 0.95668
    C. Relative child-woman ratio (24B/24A): 0.91828

25. Child-woman ratio for reference area in estimation year. — 1.03191
    A. Population aged 0-14: 3,751,000 (c)
    B. Female population 15-44: 3,635,000 (c)
    C. Child-woman ratio (25A/25B): 1.03191

26. Estimated child-woman ratio for study area in estimation year. — 0.94759
    A. Reference-area child-woman ratio in estimation year (line 25): 1.03191
    B. Relative child-woman ratio (line 24): 0.91828
    C. Estimated child-woman ratio (26A × 26B): 0.94759

27. Estimated population 0-14 for study area. — 641,058
    A. Estimated female population 15-44 (line 18): 676,518
    B. Estimated child-woman ratio (line 26): 0.94759
    C. Population estimate (27A × 27B): 641,058

Final Population Estimates

28. Total estimated population for study area. — 2,595,232
    A. Estimated population 65+ (line 6): 152,022
    B. Estimated population 45-64 (line 12): 428,351
    C. Estimated population 15-44 (line 21): 1,373,801
    D. Estimated population 0-14 (line 27): 641,058
    E. Total (28A + 28B + 28C + 28D): 2,595,232

29. Age distribution adjustment factor. — 0.99979
    A. Control total population (Chapter 4): 2,594,677
    B. Sum of age estimates (line 28): 2,595,232
    C. Adjustment factor (29A/29B): 0.99979

(continued)

Table 6-2 (Continued)

30. Adjusted estimated population by age. 2,594,677
    A. Adjustment factor (line 29): 0.99979
    B. Adjusted population 65+ (30A × line 6): 151,990
    C. Adjusted population 45-64 (30A × line 12): 428,261
    D. Adjusted population 15-44 (30A × line 21): 1,373,513
    E. Adjusted population 0-14 (30A × line 27): 640,923
    F. Total adjusted population (30B + 30C + 30D + 30E): 2,594,677

SOURCES:
(a) Bureau of the Census: decennial census.
(b) State or local health department.
(c) Federal-State Cooperative Program Agency or Census Bureau.

assuming the ratio of reference-area and study-area vital rates remains constant between 1980 and 1982, we multiply the observed census-year death rate ratio (1.20945, from line 3) by the observed estimation-year death rate for persons aged 65+ in the reference area (0.039812, from line 4). The result is the estimated study-area death rate for persons aged 65+ (0.04814). Finally, in line 6 we estimate the total population aged 65+ for the study area. Current deaths among persons aged 65+ (7,319) are divided by the estimated death rate (0.04814, from line 5) to yield the estimate of 152,022 persons aged 65+ in the study area on July 1, 1982.

An identical set of calculations is followed in lines 7-12 to produce an estimate of the study-area population aged 45-64. The result, shown on line 12, is 428,351.

We move next to the population aged 15-44, and specifically to the number of women in this group. We must develop this estimate before we can proceed to the estimates for the younger age groups, since the latter depends on the former. In line 13 we compute the fertility rate for the reference area in the census year. The rate equals the total number of births for the reference area (268,717) divided by the census count of females aged 15-44, (3,377,700).

Line 14 presents the identical calculation for the study area in the census year—50,427 births are divided by 624,566 women aged 15-44 to obtain the study-area census-year fertility rate (0.08074). In line 15 we compute the ratio of this rate to the corresponding reference-area fertility rate (0.07956, from line 13).

Line 16 shows the computation of the fertility rate for the reference area in the estimation year. The procedure is identical to that shown on lines 13 and 14; registered births (295,013) are divided by the current estimate of the reference-area female population aged 15-44 (3,635,000).

In line 17 we use this result, and the fertility-rate ratio of line 15 (1.01487), to estimate the current study-area fertility rate. Finally, in line 18 we determine the current number of women aged 15-44 in the study area. The result is 676,518.

Lines 19 and 20 show the procedure to estimate the male population aged 15-44 in the study area. In line 19 we compute the sex ratio (males/females) for persons 15-44, using counts by sex reported in the most recent census. In line 20 we multiply this ratio by the current estimate of females aged 15-44 (676,518, from line 18) to obtain the corresponding estimated male population 15-44. The result is 697,283.

Line 21 completes the estimation process for the population aged 15-44 by adding the estimated number of females in this age group (676,518) to the estimated number of males (697,283). The total is 1,373,801.

The final age group to be estimated for Harris County is the population under age 15. Since the number of deaths in this group is quite small in any one year, and fairly volatile over time even for large areas, it is better to rely on the ratio of children (aged 0-14) to women (aged 15-44) in the reference area to serve as a basis for estimating the study-area population aged 0-14. If we assume that the study-area child-woman ratio (CWR) changes over time in the same manner as the reference-area ratio, then we can use the previously determined estimate for women aged 15-44 to produce a corresponding estimate of population aged 0-14. Line 22 shows the computation of the reference-area CWR for the most recent census year. The population of both sexes under age 15 (3,518,938) is divided by the female population aged 15-44 (3,377,700). The computed CWR is 1.04181. In line 23 we use the same method to calculate the CWR for the study area in the census year. Here 597,509 children aged 0-14 are divided by 624,566 women of child-bearing age (15-44). The result is 0.95668. Line 24 illustrates the computation of the ratio of the study-area CWR to the reference-area CWR for the census year. The result, 0.91828, is the ratio of 0.95668 (line 23) to 1.04181 (line 22). In line 25 we compute the estimation-year CWR for the reference area, and in line 26 we estimate the current CWR for the study area by multiplying the census-year CWR ratio (0.91828, from line 24) by the current reference-area CWR (1.03191, from line 25). The current estimate of persons aged 0-14 in the study area is shown on line 27. The estimated female population aged 15-44 in the study area (676,518, from line 18) is multiplied by the estimated CWR (0.94759, from line 26) to obtain the result of 641,058.

The final step in the vital rates procedure for Harris County is the reconciliation of the estimates of population by age with the control-total estimate (2,594,677, from Chapter 5). On line 28 we record the sum of the four population age estimates we have just prepared: 152,022 (65+, from line 6) + 428,351 (45-64, from line 12) + 1,373,801 (15-44, from line 21) + 641,058 (0-14, from line 27). The total in question is 2,595,232. Line 29 presents an adjustment factor, which is the ratio of the control total (2,594,677) and the sum of the estimates (2,595,232, from line 28). The adjustment ratio, 0.99979, indicates that the age estimation procedure has produced an estimate of total population that slightly overstates the independent estimate from Chapter 4. Line 30 illustrates the adjustment procedure for each age estimate.

The procedure is quite simple: Multiply each age estimate by the adjustment factor (.99979) to "force" the estimated age distribution to the control total. The age estimation procedure is now complete. We have an estimate of the total resident population of Harris County, Texas on July 1, 1982, classified by broad age groups.

One final point concerns the group-quarters (nonhousehold) population. We recommend that no special adjustment be made for this category, unless (1) the size of the group-quarters population is relatively large, or (2) the number has changed significantly since the most recent census. To allow for changes in the group-quarters component, it will be necessary to obtain group-quarters figures from the most recent census that have the same demographic detail as the other population figures used in the estimation procedure. In most cases the group-quarters population is largely institutional (e.g., colleges, prisons, military installations) and heavily concentrated in only several age groups. In any event, the census-year computations for the study area should involve only the non-group-quarters (household) population, so that some adjustment to the population of lines 2, 8, 14, 19, and 23 in Table 6-2 might be needed. (Which ones should be adjusted will depend on the nature of the group-quarters population; a college dormitory with only female students, for example, would require subtracting the census count of these persons from lines 14, 19, and 23, but not 2 and 8.) The resulting estimates would apply only to the household population, so the current estimate of the group-quarters population would have to be added to the appropriate line(s) (6, 12, 18, 20, and/or 27), as well as to the control total.

APPENDIX
MAJOR SOURCES OF DEMOGRAPHIC STATISTICS

KEY

Source	*Symbol*
State Data Center	S
Federal-State Cooperative Program:	
Population Estimates	E
Population Projections	P
State Vital Statistics Office	V

Alabama

Center for Business & Economic Research (S,E,P)
University of Alabama
P.O. Box AK
University, AL 35486
(205) 348-6191

Vital Statistics (V)
Alabama Dept. of Public Health
State Office Building
Montgomery, AL 36104
(205) 832-3100

Alaska

Office of the State Demographer (S,E,P)
Department of Labor
P.O. Box 1149
Juneau, AK 99811
(907) 465-4513(S)/465-2771(E)/465-4500 (P)

Registrar of Vital Statistics (V)
Alaska Dept. of Health & Social Services
Pouch H-02G
Juneau, AK 99811
(907) 465-3111

Arizona

Arizona Department of Economic Security (S,E,P)
Population Statistics Unit 045Z
1300 West Washington, 1st Floor
P.O. Box 6123-045Z
Phoenix, AZ 85005
(602) 255-5984

Vital Records Section (V)
Arizona Dept. of Health Services
1740 West Adams Street
Phoenix, AZ 85007
(602) 255-1084

Arkansas

IREC-College of Business Administration (S,E,P)
University of Arkansas
33rd and University Avenue
Little Rock, AR 72204
(501) 371-1971

Division of Vital Statistics (V)
Arkansas Dept. of Health
4815 West Markham Street
Little Rock, AR 72201
(501) 661-2371

California

Population Research Unit (S,E,P)
Department of Finance
1025 P Street
Sacramento, CA 95814
(916) 322-4651

Vital Statistics Branch (V)
California Dept. of Health Services
410 N. Street
Sacramento, CA 95814
(916) 445-2684

Colorado

Division of Local Government (S,E,P)
Colorado Dept. of Local Affairs
1313 Sherman Street, Rm. 520
Denver, CO 80203
(303) 866-2351(S)/866-4989(E)/866-4987(P)

Health Statistics and Vital Records Division (V)
Colorado Dept. of Health
4210 East 11th Avenue
Denver, CO 80220
(303) 320-8475

Connecticut

Comprehensive Planning Division (S,P)
Office of Policy & Management
80 Washington Street
Hartford, CT 06106
(203) 566-3905

Division of Health Statistics (E,V)
Connecticut Dept. of Health Services
79 Elm Street
Hartford, CT 06115
(203) 566-5451(V)/566-3729(E)

Delaware

Delaware Development Office (S,E,P)
Townsend Building, 3rd Floor
P.O. Box 1401
Dover, DE 19901
(302) 736-4271

Chief, Vital Statistics (V)
Delaware Dept. of Health & Social Services
Jesse S. Cooper Memorial Building
Dover, DE 19901
(302) 678-4721

District of Columbia

Data Services Division (S,E,P)
Mayor's Office of Planning & Development
Rm. 458 Landsburgh Building
420 7th Street N.W.
Washington, DC 20004
(202) 727-6533(S)/727-6535 (E,P)

Vital Records Branch (V)
Research & Statistics Section
DC Dept. of Human Resources
615 Pennsylvania Avenue N.W.
Washington, DC 20001
(202) 727-5319

Florida

Division of Local Resource Management (S)
Dept. of Community Affairs
2571 Executive Center Circle East
Tallahassee, FL 32301
(904) 488-2356

Bureau of Economic & Business Research (P,E)
University of Florida
221 Matherly Hall
Gainesville, FL 32611
(904) 392-0171

Office of Vital Statistics (V)
Florida Dept. of Health & Rehabilitative Services
P.O. Box 210
Jacksonville, FL 32231
(904) 354-3961, Ext. 245

Georgia

Office of Planning & Budget (S,E)
270 Washington Street SW, Rm. 608
Atlanta, GA 30334
(404) 656-2191

Vital Records Unit (V)
Georgia Dept. of Health Resources
47 Trinity Avenue, SW
Atlanta, GA 30334
(404) 656-4750

Hawaii

Research and Economic Analysis Division (S,E,P)
Dept. of Planning & Economic Development
P.O. Box 2359
Honolulu, HI 96804
(808) 548-3017

State Registrar, Research and Statistics Office (V)
Hawaii Dept. of Health
P.O. Box 3378
Honolulu, HI 96801
(808) 548-6454

Idaho

Division of Economic & Community Affairs (S)
State Capitol Bldg., Rm. 108
Boise, ID 83720
(208) 334-3416

Division of Financial Management (E,P)
Statehouse, Rm. 122
Boise, ID 83720
(208) 334-3515

Bureau of Vital Statistics (E, V)
Idaho Dept. of Health & Welfare
700 West State Street
Boise, ID 83720
(208) 384-2493

Illinois

Division of Planning & Financial Analysis (S, P)
Illinois Bureau of the Budget
William Stratton Bldg., Rm. 605
Springfield, IL 62706
(217) 782-5414

[Vital Statistics (V)]
[Division of Health Information and Evaluation (E)]
Illinois Dept. of Public Health
535 West Jefferson Street
Springfield, IL 62761
(217) 785-2180/785-2040 (V)/785-5245 (E)

Indiana

Indiana State Library (S)
140 North Senate Avenue
Indianapolis, IN 46204
(317) 232-3735

Public Health Statistics (E,P, V)
Indiana Board of Health
1330 West Michigan Street
Indianapolis, IN 46206
(317) 633-0308

Iowa

Office of the State Demographer (S, E,P)
Iowa Office for Planning & Programming
523 East 12th Street
Des Moines, IA 50319
(515) 281-4545

Vital Records Section (V)
Iowa Dept. of Health
Robert Lucas Building
Des Moines, IA 50319
(515) 281-5871

Kansas

State Library (S)
State Capitol Bldg., Rm. 343
Topeka, KA 66612
(913) 296-3296

Division of the Budget (E,P)
Room 152 East
State House
Topeka, KA 66612
(913) 296-2826

Registration & Health Statistics (V)
Kansas Dept. of Health & Environment
6700 S. Topeka Ave., Building 321
Topeka, KA 66620
(913) 862-9360, x560/296-3527

Kentucky

Urban Studies Center (S,E,P)
University of Louisville
Gardencourt Campus
Alta Vista Road
Louisville, KY 40292
(502) 588-6626

Registrar of Vital Statistics (V)
Kentucky Dept. of Human Resources
275 East Maine Street
Frankfort, KY 40601
(502) 564-7610

Louisiana

Louisiana State Planning Office (S,P)
P.O. Box 44426
Baton Rouge, LA 70804
(504) 342-7410

Research Division (E)
College of Administration & Business
Louisiana Tech University
Ruston, LA 71272
(318) 257-3701

Registrar of Vital Statistics (V)
Louisiana Dept. of Health & Human Resources
P.O. Box 60630
New Orleans, LA 70160
(504) 568-5313

Maine

[Division of Research & Vital Records (V)]
[Division of Data And Research (E)]
Maine Dept. of Human Services
State House
Augusta, ME 04333
(207) 289-2716 (V)/289-3001 (E)

State Planning Office (P)
184 State Street
Augusta, ME 04333
(207) 289-3261

Maryland

Office of Planning Data (S,P)
Maryland Dept. of State Planning
301 West Preston Street
Baltimore, MD 21201
(301) 383-5664 (S)/383-2453 (P)

Center for Health Statistics, (E, V)
Maryland Dept. of Health & Mental Hygiene
201 West Preston Street
Baltimore, MD 21202
(301) 383-2850

Massachusetts

Center for Massachusetts Data (S,P)
Executive Office of Communities & Development
100 Cambridge Street
Boston, MA 02202
(617) 727-3253

Massachusetts Development Institute (E)
University of Massachusetts
P.O. Box 11, Thompson Hall
Amherst MA 01003
(413) 549-4930 x 234

Office of State Health Planning (V)
Massachusetts Dept. of Public Health
600 Washington Street, Rm. 614
Boston, MA 02111
(617) 727-4164

Michigan

Michigan Information Center (S, E,P)
Department of Management & Budget
Office of the Budget/LLPD
P.O. Box 30026
Lansing, MI 48909
(517) 373-7910

Deputy Director (V)
Michigan Dept. of Public Health
3500 N. Logan Street
P.O. Box 30035
Lansing, MI 48914
(517) 373-1322

Minnesota

State Demographic Unit (S, E, P)
Minnesota Dept. of Energy, Planning & Development
101 Capitol Square Building
550 Cedar Street
St. Paul, MN 55101
(612) 297-2557

Center for Health Statistics (V)
Minnesota Dept. of Health
717 Delaware Street, SE
Minneapolis, MN 55440
(612) 296-5358

Mississippi

Center for Population Studies (S)
University of Mississippi
Bondurant Building, Rm. 3W
University, MS 38677
(601) 232-7288

Mississippi Research and Development Center (E,P)
Economic Analysis Division
P.O. Drawer 2470
Jackson, MS 39205
(601) 982-6408(E)/982-6456(P)

Missouri

Missouri State Library (S)
P.O. Box 387
Jefferson City, MO 65102
(314) 751-4552

Office of Administration (E,P)
Missouri Division of Planning & Budget
P.O. Box 809
Capitol Building, Rm. 129
Jefferson City, MO 65102
(314) 751-2345(E)/751-2073(P)

Center for Health Statistics (V)
Missouri Dept. of Health
Broadway State Office Building
309 Adams Street
Jefferson City, MO 65101
(314) 751-2713

Montana

Census & Economic Information Center (S)
Montana Dept. of Administration
Capitol Station
Mitchell Building, Rm. 108
Helena, MT 59620
(406) 449-2896

Bureau of Business & Economic Research (E)
University of Montana
Missoula, MT 59812
(406) 243-5113

Bureau of Records & Statistics (V)
Montana Dept. of Health & Environmental Sciences
Helena, MT 59601
(406) 449-2614

Nebraska

Bureau of Business Research (S,E)
200 CBA
University of Nebraska—Lincoln
Lincoln, NE 68588
(402) 472-2334

Policy Research Office (P)
P.O. Box 94601
State Capitol
Lincoln, NE 68509
(402) 471-2414

Division of Health Data & Statistical Research (V)
Nebraska Dept. of Health
State Office Building
301 Centennial Mall South
Lincoln, NE 68509
(402) 471-2241

Nevada

Nevada State Library (S)
Capitol Complex
401 North Carson
Carson City, NV 89710
(702) 885-5160

Bureau of Business and Economic Research (E)
College of Business Administration
University of Nevada
Reno, NV 89577
(702) 784-6877

Office of the State Planning Coordinator (P)
Capitol Complex
Carson City, NV 89710
(702) 885-4865

Section of Vital Statistics (V)
Division of Health
Nevada Dept. of Human Resources
Capitol Complex, Kenhead Building, Rm. 102
505 East King Street
Carson City, NV 89710
(702) 885-4480

New Hampshire

Office of State Planning (S,E,P)
2½ Beacon Street
Concord, NH 03301
(603) 271-2155

Bureau of Vital Records & Health Statistics (V)
New Hampshire Division of Public Health
Health and Welfare Building
Hazen Drive
Concord, NH 03301
(603) 271-4654

New Jersey

New Jersey Department of Labor (S,E,P)
Division of Planning & Research
P.O. Box 845/CN 388
Trenton, NJ 08625-0388
(609) 984-2593(S)/292-0076(E)/292-0099(P)

Division of Health Planning and Resources Development (V)
New Jersey Dept. of Public Health
P.O. Box 1540
Trenton, NJ 08625
(609) 292-5960

New Mexico

New Mexico Department of Finance & Administration (S)
421 State Capitol Building
Sante Fe, NM 87503
(505) 827-2665

Bureau of Business & Economic Research (E,P)
University of New Mexico
Albuquerque, NM 87131
(505) 277-2216

State Registrar (V)
New Mexico Health Agency
Health & Social Services Dept.
P.O. Box 2348
Santa Fe, NM 87501
(505) 827-2588

New York

Division of Economic Research & Statistics (S,E,P)
New York Department of Commerce
Twin Towers, Rm. 1005
99 Washington Avenue
Albany, NY 12245
(518) 474-6115

Population Research Section (E,P)
Department of City Planning
2 Lafayette Street, Rm. 2107
New York, NY 10007
(New York City data)

Director of Health Statistics (V)
New York State Dept. of Health & Health Resources
Empire State Plaza, Tower Building
Albany, NY 12237
(518) 474-8260

Bureau of Vital Records (V)
New York City Dept. of Health
125 Worth St.
New York, NY 10013
(212) 566-8193
(New York City data)

North Carolina

Office of State Budget and Management (S, E,P)
North Carolina Department of Administration
116 West Jones Street
Raleigh, NC 27611
(919) 733-7061

Vital Records Branch (V)
North Carolina Division of Health Services
P.O. Box 2091
Raleigh, NC 27602
(919) 733-3000

North Dakota

Department of Agricultural Economics (S)
North Dakota State University
Agricultural Experiment Station
Morrill Hall, Rm. 207
P.O. Box 5636
Fargo, ND 58105
(701) 237-7400

Office of Statistical Services (E, V)
North Dakota Dept. of Health
State Capitol, 1st Floor, Judicial Wing
Bismarck, ND 58505
(701) 224-4508

State Planning (P)
State Capitol
Bismarck, ND 58505
(701) 224-2818

Ohio

Ohio Data Users Center (S,E,P)
Department of Economic & Community Development
P.O. Box 1001
Columbus, OH 43216
(614) 466-7772/2115/3379

Division of Vital Statistics (V)
Ohio Dept. of Health
450 E. Town Street
P.O. Box 118
Columbus, OH 43216
(614) 466-2533

Oklahoma

Oklahoma State Data Center (S,P)
Dept. of Economic and Community Affairs
Lincoln Plaza Building, Suite 285
4545 North Lincoln Boulevard
Oklahoma City, OK 73105
(405) 528-8200(S)/521-4545(P)

Research & Planning (E)
Oklahoma Employment Security Commission
310 Will Rogers Building
Oklahoma City, OK 73105
(405) 521-3735

Division of Data Management (V)
Oklahoma Dept. of Health
N.E. 10th& Stonewall
P.O. Box 53551
Oklahoma City, OK 73105
(405) 271-4542

Oregon

Intergovernmental Relations Div. (S)
Executive Building
155 Cottage Street, NE
Salem, OR 97310
(503) 373-1996

Center for Population Research & Census (E,P)
Portland State University
P.O. Box 751
Portland, OR 97207
(503) 229-3922

State Registrar (V)
Oregon Health Division
P.O. Box 231
Portland, OR 97207
(503) 229-5896

Pennsylvania

Institute of State and Regional Affairs (S,E)
Pennsylvania State University
Capitol Campus
Middletown, PA 17057
(717) 948-6336

BMS, Office of Budget Administration (P)
Governor's Office
903 Health & Welfare Building
Harrisburg, PA 17120
(717) 787-6303

Division of Health Statistics (V)
Pennsylvania Dept. of Health
P.O. Box 90
Harrisburg, PA 17120
(717) 783-3218

Puerto Rico

Puerto Rico Planning Board (S, E)
Minallas Governmnt Center
North Building, Avenida de Diego
P.O. Box 41119
San Juan, PR 00940
(809) 726-5020

Puerto Rico Health Statistics System (V)
Puerto Rico Dept. of Health
Box 9342
Santurce, PR 00908
(809) 782-0120

Rhode Island

Rhode Island Statewide Planning Program (S, E,P)
265 Melrose Street, Rm. 203
Providence, RI 02907
(401) 277-2656

Division of Vital Statistics (V)
Rhode Island Dept. of Health
Health Building
Davis Street
Providence, RI 02908
(401) 277-2811

South Carolina

Division of Research & Statistical Services (S,E,P)
Budget & Control Board
Rembert C. Dennis Bldg.
1000 Assembly Street
Columbia, SC 29201
(803) 758-3986

Division of Vital Records (V)
South Carolina Dept. of Health & Environmental Control
2600 Bull Street
Columbia, SC 29201
(803) 758-5511

South Dakota

Business Research Bureau (S)
School Of Business, Patterson Hall
University of South Dakota
Vermillion, SD 57069
(605) 677-5287

Planning Information Section (P)
State Planning Bureau
State Capitol
Pierre, SD 57501
(605) 773-3661

Center for Health Statistics (E,V)
South Dakota Dept. of Health
Joe Foss Building
Pierre, SD 57501
(605) 773-3355

Tennessee

Tennessee State Planning Office (S,E)
James K. Polk State Office Building
505 Deadrick Street, Suite 1800
Nashville, TN 37219
(615) 741-1676

Center for Business and Economic Research (P)
University of Tennessee
Room 100, Glocker Hall
Knoxville, TN 37916
(615) 974-5441

Center for Health Statistics (V)
Tennessee Dept. of Public Health
Room 320, Capitol Hill Building
301 7th Avenue, N.W.
Nashville, TN 37219
(615) 741-1954/7213

Texas

Texas 2000 (S,E,P)
Governor's Office of Budget & Planning
P.O. Box 13561
Austin, TX 78711
(512) 475-8386

Bureau of Vital Statistics (V)
Texas Dept. of Health Resources
1100 West 49th Street
Austin, TX 78756
(512) 458-7692

Utah

State Planning Coordinator's Office (S,E,P)
State Capitol, Rm. 124
Salt Lake City, UT 84114
(801) 533-4659/5245

Bureau of Vital Statistics (V)
Utah Division of Health
44 Medical Drive
Salt Lake City, UT 84113
(801) 533-6186

Vermont

Vermont State Planning Office (S)
Pavilion Office Building
109 State Street
Montpelier, VT 05602
(802) 828-3326

[Population Estimation/Projection Program (E,P)]
[Division of Public Health Statistics (V)]
Vermont Dept. of Health
115 Colchester Avenue
Burlington, VT 05401
(802) 862-5701

Virginia

Dept. of Planning & Budget (S,P)
445 Ninth Street Office Building
P.O. Box 1422
Richmond, VA 23211
(804) 786-7843

Tayloe Murphy Institute (E)
University of Virginia
Dynamics Building, 4th Floor
2015 Ivy Road
Charlottesville, VA 22903
(804) 971-2661

Center for Health Statistics (V)
Virginia Dept. of Health
James Madison Building
P.O. Box 1000
Richmond, VA 23219
(804) 786-6206

Washington

Forecasting & Estimation Division (S,E,P)
Office of Financial Management
400 East Union, Mail Stop ER-13
Olympia, WA 98504
(206) 753-5617

Center for Health Statistics (V)
Washington Dept. of Social & Health Services
Mail Stop OB-44J
Olympia, WA 98504
(206) 753-5882

West Virginia

Community Development Division (S,P)
Governor's Office of Economic & Community Development
Capitol Complex, Building 6, Rm. 553
Charleston, WV 25305
(304) 348-4010(S)/348-2246(P)

Office of Research and Development (E)
West Virginia University
404 Knapp Hall
Morgantown, WV 26506
(304) 293-4201

Registration and Vital Statistics (V)
West Virginia Dept. of Health
1800 Washington Street East
Charleston, WV 25305
(304) 348-2971

Wisconsin

Demographic Services Center (S)
Wisconsin Dept. of Administration
101 South Webster Street, 7th Floor
P.O. Box 7864
Madison, WI 53707
(608) 266-1927

Section of Demographic & Special Analysis (E,P,V)
Bureau of Health Statistics
Wisconsin Dept. of Health
P.O. Box 309
Madison, WI 53701
(608) 266-1920 (E,P)/266-1334 (V)

Wyoming

Institute for Policy Research (E)
University of Wyoming
University Station
Box 3925
Laramie, WY 82071
(307) 766-5141

Division of Research and Statistics (P)
Wyoming Dept. of Administration and Financial Control
Emerson Building
Cheyenne, WY 82001
(307) 777-7201

Vital Records Services (V)
Wyoming Dept. of Health & Medical Services
Hathaway Building
Cheyenne, WY 82002
(307) 777-7591/7121

NOTES

1. The designation "county equivalent" applies to the primary substate divisions of Alaska and Louisiana; to 44 cities that are independent of any county (Baltimore, Maryland; St. Louis, Missouri; Carson City, Nevada; and 41 cities in Virginia); and to the Montana portion of Yellowstone National Park. Neither Alaska nor Louisiana has principal subdivisions that are formally called counties. The more populous areas of Alaska are divided into boroughs, and with the help of the Census Bureau, the balance of the state now has been divided into special "census areas." In Louisiana the principal subdivision of the state is called a parish, following the region's strong French traditions, and the Census Bureau considers these units county equivalents.

2. At any time between decennial enumerations, a local government may request the Census Bureau to conduct a special census. The responsibility for these censuses rests with the network of bureau regional offices. Conducted under guidelines promulgated by the Census Bureau, special censuses typically focus on counting population and contain only a few of the basic (100 percent) subject items found on the decennial schedule.

REFERENCES

American Statistical Association (1977) Report on the Conference on Economic and Demographic Methods for Projecting Population. Washington, DC: Author.

ATCHLEY, R. (1968) "A short-cut method for estimating the population of metropolitan areas." Journal of the American Institute of Planners 34: 259-262.

BOGUE, D. (1950) "A technique for making extensive population estimates." Journal of the American Statistical Association 45: 149-163.

CAVANAUGH, F. J. (1981) "The Census Bureau's 1980 census test of population estimates," pp. 3-11 in Small-Area Population Estimates—Methods and their Accuracy. Small Area Statistics Papers, Series GE-41, No. 7. Washington, DC: U.S. Bureau of Census.

ERICKSEN, E. (1974) "A regression method for estimating population changes of local areas." Journal of the American Statistical Association 69: 867-875.

GONZALES, M. and C. HOZA (1978) "Small area estimation with applications to unemployment and housing estimates." Journal of the American Statistical Association 73: 7-15.

GREENBERG, M.R., D. A. KRUECKEBERG, and C. O. MICHAELSON (1978) Local Population and Employment Projection Techniques. New Brunswick, NJ: Center for Urban Policy Research, Rutgers University.

HAMILTON, C. and J. PERRY (1962) "A short method for projecting population by age from one decennial census to another." Social Forces 41: 163-170.

IRWIN, R. (1977) Guide for Local Area Population Projections. Technical Paper No. 39. Washington, DC: U.S. Bureau of the Census.

ISSERMAN, A. (1977) "The accuracy of population projections for subcounty areas." Journal of the American Institute of Planners 43: 247-259.

KEYFITZ, N. (1981) "The limits of population forecasting." Population and Development Review 7: 579-593.

———(1972) "On future population." Journal of the American Statistical Association 67: 347-363.

LEE, E. and H. GOLDSMITH [eds.] (1982) Population Estimates: Methods for Small Area Analysis. Beverly Hills, CA: Sage.

LEVY, P. (1979) "Small area estimates—synthetic and other procedures, 1968-1978," pp. 4-19 in J. Steinberg (ed.) Synthetic Estimates for Small Areas. Rockville, MD: National Institute on Drug Abuse.

MANDELL, M. and J. TAYMAN (1982) "Measuring temporal stability in regression models of population estimation." Demography 19: 135-146.

MARTIN, J. and W. SEROW (1978) "Estimating demographic characteristics using the ratio-correlation method." Demography 15: 223-233.

MORRISON, P. and D. RELLES (1975) "A method for monitoring small-area population changes in cities." Review of Public Data Use 3: 10-15.

NAMBOODIRI, N. (1972) "On the ratio-correlation and related methods of subnational population estimation." Demography 9: 443-453.

National Research Council (1980) Estimating Population and Income of Small Areas. Washington, DC: National Academy Press.

Oak Ridge Associated Universities (1977) Population Forecasting for Small Areas. Oak Ridge, TN: Author.

O'HARE, W. (1976) "Report on a multiple regression method for making population estimates." Demography 13: 369-379.

PITTENGER, D. (1976) Projecting State and Local Populations. Cambridge, MD: Ballinger.

PURSELL, D. (1970) "Improving population estimates with the use of dummy variables." Demography 7: 87-91.

RIVES, N. (1976) "A modified housing unit method for small area population estimation." Proceedings of the American Statistical Association, Social Statistics Section: 717-720.

ROSENBERG, H. (1968) "Improving current population estimates through stratification." Land Economics 44: 331-338.

SCHAIBLE, W., D. BROCK, and G. SCHNACK (1977) "An empirical comparison of the simple inflation, synthetic and composite estimators for small area statistics." Proceedings of the American Statistical Association, Social Statistics Section: 1017-1021.

SCHMITT, R. and A. CROSETTI (1954) "Accuracy of the ratio-correlation method for estimating postcensal population." Land Economics 30: 279-281.

SHRYOCK, H., J. SIEGEL, and Associates (1976) The Methods and Materials of Demography (condensed edition by E. Stockwell). New York: Academic Press.

SMITH, S. and B. LEWIS (1980) "Some new techniques for applying the housing unit method of local population estimation." Demography 17: 323-339.

SPAR, M. and J. MARTIN (1979) "Refinements to regression-based estimates of postcensal population characteristics." Review of Public Data Use 7: 16-22.

STARSINIC, D. and M. ZITTER (1968) "Accuracy of the housing unit method in preparing population estimates for cities." Demography 5: 475-484.

STOTO, M. (1983) "The accurcy of population projections." Journal of the American Statistical Association 78: 13-20.

SUMMERS, A. and B. WOLFE (1978) "Estimating household income from location." Journal of the American Statistical Association 73: 288-292.

SWANSON, D. (1978) "An evaluation of 'ratio' and 'difference' regression methods for estimating small, highly concentrated populations: the case of ethnic groups." Review of Public Data Use 6: 18-27.

U.S. Bureau of the Census (1980a) Census '80: Continuing the Factfinder Tradition. Washington, DC: Author.

———(1980b) Population and Per Capita Money Income Estimates for Local Areas: Detailed Methodology and Evaluation. Current Population Reports, Series P-25, No. 699. Washington, DC: Author.

———(1979a) Twenty Censuses: Population and Housing Questions, 1790-1980. Washington, DC: Author.

———(1979b) Illustrative Projections of State Populations by Age, Race, and Sex: 1975-2000. Current Population Reports, Series P-25, No. 796. Washington, DC: Author.

———(1974) Estimates of Coverage of Population by Sex, Race, and Age: Demographic Analysis. Census of Population and Housing: 1970, Evaluation and Research Program Report PHC (E)-4. Washington, DC: Author.

———(1973) Federal-State Cooperative Program for Local Population Estimates: Test Results April 1, 1970. Current Population Reports, Series P-26, No. 21. Washington, DC: Author.

ZITTER, M. and H. SHRYOCK (1964) "Accuracy of methods of preparing postcensal population estimates for states and local areas." Demography 1: 227-241.

NORFLEET W. RIVES, Jr., is Associate Professor in the College of Urban Affairs and Public Policy and the Department of Mathematical Sciences at the University of Delaware. He received his Ph.D. in economics from Duke. During part of the preparation of this volume he was a visiting fellow in demography at Rice Center, the community research and development corporation of Rice University. His research interests include small-area demographic measurement and business applications of demography.

WILLIAM J. SEROW is Professor of Economics and Research Associate in the Center for the Study of Population at Florida State University. He received his Ph.D. in economics from Duke University. His research interests include the economics and demography of aging, migration, and small-area demography.